The Essential Guide to Mental Health Coaching: Empowerment and Wellness

Laurel D. Malvern

"The Essential Guide to Mental Health Coaching:
Empowerment and Wellness"

Preface

Welcome to "The Essential Guide to Mental Health Coaching: Empowerment and Wellness." In today's dynamic world, the pursuit of mental well-being is more crucial than ever. As a seasoned mental health coach, I have witnessed firsthand the transformative power of coaching in enhancing individuals' lives.

This book is a culmination of my years of experience, research, and passion for empowering others through mental health coaching. It aims to serve as a comprehensive resource for both aspiring coaches and individuals seeking to understand and harness the benefits of mental health coaching.

Why This Book?

Mental health coaching is not just a profession; it is a calling to support and uplift individuals on their journey towards resilience, growth, and fulfillment. Through these pages, I aim to demystify the complexities of mental health coaching, offering practical insights, evidence-based strategies, and ethical considerations essential for effective practice.

What You'll Find Inside

Each chapter of this book is designed to equip you with the knowledge and tools needed to navigate various aspects of mental health coaching:

- Understanding the foundational principles and evolution of mental health coaching.
- Exploring the roles, responsibilities, and ethical standards that guide professional practice.
- Integrating psychological theories, neuroscience insights, and innovative techniques into coaching sessions.
- Addressing specific mental health challenges with compassion and expertise.
- Cultivating personal growth, resilience, and emotional intelligence through coaching.
- Navigating cultural diversity and technological advancements in the field.
- Looking ahead to the future trends and possibilities in mental health coaching.

A Call to Action

As you embark on this journey through "The Essential Guide to Mental Health Coaching," I invite you to approach each chapter with curiosity and a commitment to learning. Whether you are a coach, client, or simply curious about mental health coaching, my hope is that this book serves as a valuable resource and inspires meaningful conversations about mental well-being.

Thank you for joining me on this transformative exploration of mental health coaching. Together, we can foster empowerment, wellness, and resilience in ourselves and others.

Warm regards,

Laurel D. Malvern

Introduction: Overview of the Importance of Mental Health Coaching

In the increasingly complex landscape of modern life, mental health has emerged as a critical component of overall well-being. From the pressures of career and relationships to the pervasive influence of digital connectivity, individuals face a myriad of challenges that can impact their mental and emotional health. In response to these challenges, mental health coaching has risen to prominence as a proactive and empowering approach to support individuals in navigating these complexities.

Mental health coaching is distinct from traditional therapy or counseling in its focus on personal growth, goal achievement, and enhancing resilience. It empowers individuals to take an active role in managing their mental health by providing them with practical tools, strategies, and support. By blending the principles of coaching with insights from psychology and neuroscience, mental health coaches help clients identify and leverage their strengths, cultivate self-awareness, and develop effective coping mechanisms.

At its core, mental health coaching fosters a collaborative partnership between coach and client, built on trust, empathy, and mutual respect. Through structured sessions and personalized guidance, coaches assist clients in clarifying their goals, overcoming obstacles, and achieving sustainable changes in their lives. Whether addressing challenges like stress management, anxiety, depression, or navigating life transitions, mental health coaching offers a holistic approach that considers the interconnected aspects of an individual's life.

This book serves as a comprehensive guide to understanding and practicing mental health coaching effectively. It explores the foundational principles of coaching, ethical considerations, and the qualifications necessary for effective practice. Chapters delve into the integration of psychological theories and neuroscience research, providing evidence-based strategies for enhancing mental well-being. Practical techniques such as Cognitive Behavioral Coaching (CBC), Positive Psychology interventions, and mindfulness-based approaches are examined in depth, along with their applications in addressing specific mental health challenges.

Through case studies, real-world examples, and insights from experienced coaches, readers will gain a deep understanding of how mental health coaching can empower individuals to thrive in all aspects of their lives. We will also explore the importance of cultural sensitivity in coaching, ethical guidelines, and the integration of technology in enhancing coaching outcomes.

Join me on this transformative journey as we explore the profound impact of mental health coaching and empower individuals to cultivate resilience, achieve personal growth, and embrace a life of wellness and fulfillment.

Chapter 1: What is mental health coaching, and how does it differ from therapy and counseling?

Mental health coaching, therapy, and counseling are distinct approaches to supporting individuals' mental and emotional well-being, each with its own focus and methodologies:

Mental Health Coaching:

Focus: Mental health coaching primarily focuses on personal growth, goal-setting, and achieving positive behavioral changes. It emphasizes empowering individuals to enhance their overall well-being, manage stress, improve self-confidence, and achieve personal goals.
Methodology: Coaches use a collaborative and strengths-based approach, often drawing from techniques rooted in positive psychology, cognitive-behavioral principles, mindfulness practices, and other evidence-based strategies. Sessions are forward-looking, focusing on the present and future rather than delving deeply into past traumas or unresolved issues.
Therapy:

Focus: Therapy, also known as psychotherapy or counseling, focuses on diagnosing and treating mental health disorders, emotional difficulties, and psychological issues. It aims to alleviate symptoms, heal past wounds, and explore underlying causes of distress or dysfunction.

Methodology: Therapists are trained in various therapeutic modalities (e.g., psychoanalysis, cognitive-behavioral therapy, humanistic therapy) tailored to specific conditions and client needs. Therapy sessions often involve deeper exploration of emotions, thoughts, and behavioral patterns, aiming for long-term emotional and psychological healing.

Counseling:

Focus: Counseling typically focuses on addressing specific issues, improving interpersonal relationships, and providing guidance during life transitions or crises. It can encompass a wide range of areas, including career counseling, marriage counseling, grief counseling, and more.

Methodology: Counselors use supportive techniques, problem-solving strategies, and sometimes brief therapeutic interventions to help clients resolve immediate concerns, gain clarity, and make informed decisions.

Key Differences:

Goal Orientation: Mental health coaching focuses on achieving specific goals, personal growth, and enhancing overall well-being, whereas therapy and counseling often aim to alleviate symptoms of mental health disorders or address specific psychological issues.

Time Frame: Coaching sessions are typically shorter-term and goal-oriented, focusing on practical strategies and solutions for current challenges. In contrast, therapy and counseling sessions may be longer-term and involve deeper exploration of past experiences and emotions.

Scope of Practice: Coaches do not diagnose or treat mental health disorders, whereas therapists and counselors are trained and licensed to diagnose and provide treatment for psychological conditions.

Client-Centered Approach: Coaching empowers clients to drive their own personal development and change process, while therapy and counseling often involve more direct guidance and therapeutic interventions from the practitioner.

In essence, while all three disciplines aim to improve mental and emotional well-being, they vary significantly in their focus, approach, and scope of practice, catering to different needs and objectives of individuals seeking support for their mental health concerns.

Chapter 2: What qualifications and certifications are necessary to become a mental health coach?

Becoming a mental health coach involves acquiring specific qualifications and certifications that ensure competence in supporting individuals' mental and emotional well-being. While the requirements can vary based on location and specific coaching niches, here are general qualifications and certifications typically sought after to become a mental health coach:

Education and Training:

Bachelor's Degree: While not always mandatory, many mental health coaches have a bachelor's degree in psychology, counseling, social work, or a related field. This educational background provides foundational knowledge in human behavior, mental health concepts, and ethical considerations. Master's Degree (Optional): Some mental health coaches pursue a master's degree in counseling, psychology, or a related field to deepen their understanding of mental health theories and therapeutic techniques. A master's degree can enhance credibility and provide advanced training in clinical practice.
Coaching Training Programs:

Completion of accredited coaching training programs is essential. Look for programs approved by reputable coaching organizations like the International Coach Federation (ICF), which sets industry standards and offers accreditation to coaching programs that meet their criteria.

These training programs typically cover coaching principles, techniques, ethics, and practical skills necessary to work effectively with clients.

Certification:

ICF Certification: The International Coach Federation (ICF) is a globally recognized accrediting body for coaches. Coaches can pursue different levels of certification (Associate Certified Coach, Professional Certified Coach, Master Certified Coach) by meeting specific training hours, coaching experience, and passing a rigorous examination.

Other Certifications: In addition to ICF certification, there are other specialized certifications relevant to mental health coaching, such as certifications in positive psychology coaching, cognitive-behavioral coaching, or mindfulness coaching. These certifications demonstrate expertise in specific coaching approaches and techniques.

Supervised Experience:

Gaining supervised coaching experience under the guidance of experienced coaches or mentors is valuable. This practical experience allows new coaches to apply theoretical knowledge, refine coaching skills, and build confidence in working with clients.

Continuing Education and Professional Development:

Mental health coaching is a dynamic field, and ongoing learning is essential to stay updated with new research, trends, and best practices. Coaches should engage in continuing education, attend workshops, conferences, and pursue advanced training to enhance their coaching skills and knowledge.
Ethical Guidelines and Standards:

Understanding and adhering to ethical guidelines and professional standards is crucial for maintaining integrity and trust in coaching practice. Coaches should familiarize themselves with ethical codes set by coaching organizations and adhere to confidentiality, boundaries, and client welfare principles.
By acquiring these qualifications and certifications, mental health coaches demonstrate their commitment to professional excellence, ethical practice, and ongoing professional development, ensuring they are well-equipped to support clients effectively in achieving their mental health and well-being goals.

Chapter 3: How can mental health coaching help individuals manage anxiety, stress, and other mental health challenges?

Mental health coaching offers effective strategies and support for individuals dealing with anxiety, stress, and various mental health challenges. Here are several ways in which mental health coaching can help:

Holistic Approach: Mental health coaching takes a holistic approach to wellness, addressing the interconnected aspects of an individual's life, including physical, emotional, social, and spiritual dimensions. Coaches work with clients to identify underlying causes of anxiety and stress, such as lifestyle factors, thought patterns, and environmental triggers.

Goal Setting and Action Planning: Coaches collaborate with clients to set clear, achievable goals related to managing anxiety and stress. These goals may include developing healthy coping mechanisms, improving time management, practicing relaxation techniques, or enhancing communication skills.

Cognitive Behavioral Techniques: Cognitive Behavioral Coaching (CBC) techniques are often employed to help clients identify and challenge negative thought patterns and beliefs that contribute to anxiety and stress. Coaches teach practical strategies to reframe thoughts, manage emotions, and cultivate a more positive mindset.

Mindfulness and Relaxation Practices: Coaches integrate mindfulness-based approaches and relaxation techniques into sessions to promote awareness, reduce physiological arousal, and enhance stress resilience. Techniques such as deep breathing exercises, guided imagery, and progressive muscle relaxation can be taught to manage acute stress responses.

Building Resilience: Mental health coaching focuses on building resilience, which involves developing adaptive coping skills and the ability to bounce back from setbacks. Coaches help clients strengthen their resilience through goal-oriented actions, self-reflection, and learning from challenging experiences.

Accountability and Support: Coaches provide a supportive and non-judgmental environment where clients can openly discuss their concerns and progress. Regular coaching sessions offer accountability, encouragement, and feedback to help individuals stay motivated and committed to their goals.

Lifestyle Modification: Coaches emphasize the importance of lifestyle factors such as nutrition, exercise, sleep hygiene, and social support networks in managing anxiety and stress. They work with clients to identify areas for improvement and implement sustainable changes that promote overall well-being.

Empowerment and Self-Efficacy: Through the coaching process, individuals gain a sense of empowerment and self-efficacy as they develop skills and strategies to effectively manage their mental health challenges. Coaches encourage clients to take proactive steps towards their goals and celebrate their successes along the way.

Long-Term Support and Maintenance: Mental health coaching provides ongoing support and guidance, helping individuals maintain their progress and navigate potential setbacks or relapses. Coaches empower clients with tools and strategies they can continue to use independently to promote lasting change.

Overall, mental health coaching offers a personalized and proactive approach to managing anxiety, stress, and other mental health challenges. By focusing on empowerment, skill-building, and holistic well-being, coaches help individuals cultivate resilience, improve their quality of life, and achieve sustainable mental health outcomes.

Chapter 4: What role does neuroscience play in mental health coaching, and how can it inform coaching practices?

Neuroscience plays a significant role in enhancing the effectiveness of mental health coaching by providing insights into brain function, behavior change mechanisms, and the physiological basis of mental health challenges. Here's how neuroscience informs coaching practices:

Understanding Brain Function:

Neuroplasticity: Neuroscience research shows that the brain has the ability to change and adapt throughout life, known as neuroplasticity. Coaches utilize this knowledge to help clients rewire neural pathways associated with negative thought patterns, habits, and behaviors. By engaging in targeted exercises and cognitive strategies, clients can reshape their brain's response to stressors and enhance emotional regulation.
Behavior Change Mechanisms:

Reward Pathways: Neuroscience identifies reward pathways in the brain linked to motivation, goal achievement, and positive reinforcement. Coaches leverage this understanding to structure coaching sessions that set achievable goals, provide incremental rewards for progress, and reinforce desired behaviors. This approach encourages clients to stay motivated and committed to their mental health goals.
Emotion Regulation:

Amygdala and Prefrontal Cortex: The amygdala, responsible for processing emotions, interacts with the prefrontal cortex, involved in decision-making and impulse control. Coaches educate clients on these brain regions' roles and teach techniques such as mindfulness, deep breathing, and cognitive reframing to regulate emotional responses effectively. This knowledge helps clients manage anxiety, stress, and emotional volatility by enhancing self-awareness and self-regulation skills.
Stress Response and Resilience:

Hypothalamic-Pituitary-Adrenal (HPA) Axis: Neuroscience studies the HPA axis, which regulates the body's stress response through the release of cortisol and other hormones. Coaches educate clients on the physiological effects of chronic stress and teach stress management techniques that mitigate HPA axis activation. Strategies such as relaxation techniques, physical exercise, and positive coping mechanisms help clients build resilience and minimize the impact of stress on mental health.
Neuroscience-Informed Techniques:

Mindfulness-Based Interventions: Coaches integrate mindfulness practices informed by neuroscience research to cultivate present-moment awareness, reduce rumination, and promote stress reduction. Mindfulness techniques enhance cognitive flexibility, emotional regulation, and overall psychological well-being, making them valuable tools in coaching sessions.

Cognitive Behavioral Techniques: Neuroscience supports the effectiveness of Cognitive Behavioral Coaching (CBC) techniques, which focus on identifying and modifying cognitive distortions and behavioral patterns contributing to mental health challenges. Coaches use evidence-based strategies to help clients challenge negative thinking, develop realistic perspectives, and adopt healthier coping strategies.

Personalized Coaching Approaches:

Individual Differences: Neuroscience underscores the importance of personalized coaching approaches that consider individual differences in brain structure, function, and genetic predispositions. Coaches tailor interventions to match clients' unique cognitive styles, learning preferences, and emotional responses, optimizing coaching outcomes and client engagement.

By integrating neuroscience insights into coaching practices, mental health coaches can offer evidence-based interventions that promote neuroplasticity, enhance emotional regulation, and support long-term mental health and well-being. This approach not only empowers clients with scientific knowledge but also fosters resilience and sustainable behavior change essential for maintaining optimal mental health.

Chapter 5: How can cultural sensitivity be integrated into mental health coaching practices?

Integrating cultural sensitivity into mental health coaching practices is crucial for effectively supporting clients from diverse cultural backgrounds. Here are several strategies to ensure cultural sensitivity in coaching:

Cultural Awareness and Education:

Coaches should educate themselves about the cultural backgrounds, values, beliefs, and norms of their clients. This involves learning about different cultural practices, communication styles, family dynamics, and socio-economic factors that may influence clients' perspectives on mental health and well-being.
Respect for Diversity:

Coaches should demonstrate respect for cultural diversity and acknowledge the uniqueness of each client's cultural identity. This includes avoiding assumptions based on stereotypes and recognizing that cultural experiences shape individuals' perceptions, behaviors, and coping strategies.
Building Trust and Rapport:

Establishing trust and rapport is essential in coaching relationships. Coaches should create a safe and non-judgmental space where clients feel comfortable discussing cultural concerns, experiences of discrimination, or challenges related to acculturation. Active listening and empathy are key to understanding clients' cultural contexts.
Tailoring Coaching Approaches:

Coaches should adapt their coaching approaches to align with clients' cultural preferences and values. This may involve modifying coaching techniques, goal-setting processes, and communication styles to resonate with clients' cultural norms and expectations. Flexibility and openness to cultural differences enhance the relevance and effectiveness of coaching interventions.
Addressing Cultural Stigma and Mental Health Taboos:

In many cultures, there may be stigma surrounding mental health issues or reluctance to seek professional help. Coaches can play a role in reducing stigma by promoting awareness, normalizing discussions about mental health, and highlighting the benefits of coaching as a supportive resource.
Collaborative Goal Setting:

Coaches should collaborate with clients to set culturally appropriate and meaningful goals that align with their cultural values and aspirations. This involves understanding how cultural identity influences clients' priorities, life goals, and definitions of success.
Cultural Humility and Continuous Learning:

Adopting a stance of cultural humility involves recognizing one's own cultural biases and limitations while remaining open to learning from clients' cultural perspectives. Coaches should engage in ongoing self-reflection, seek feedback from clients, and pursue professional development opportunities to enhance cultural competence.
Seeking Consultation and Collaboration:

When working with clients from cultural backgrounds different from their own, coaches may benefit from consulting with colleagues, cultural advisors, or mental health professionals with expertise in cross-cultural issues. Collaboration ensures that coaching practices remain culturally responsive and inclusive.
By integrating cultural sensitivity into mental health coaching practices, coaches can foster trust, enhance client engagement, and promote positive outcomes that respect and honor clients' cultural identities and experiences. This approach contributes to a more inclusive and effective coaching process that acknowledges the diverse needs and strengths of all clients.

Chapter 6: What ethical considerations should mental health coaches be aware of, and how can they maintain professional standards?

Mental health coaches must adhere to ethical guidelines to ensure the well-being and trust of their clients. Here are key ethical considerations and strategies for maintaining professional standards in mental health coaching:

Confidentiality:

Coaches should prioritize client confidentiality, maintaining strict boundaries regarding the disclosure of client information. Confidentiality builds trust and allows clients to share openly without fear of privacy breaches. Coaches must inform clients about the limits of confidentiality, such as mandated reporting laws in cases of imminent harm.
Informed Consent:

Coaches should obtain informed consent from clients before beginning coaching engagements. Informed consent involves explaining the coaching process, goals, roles, expectations, fees, and confidentiality policies in clear and understandable terms. Clients should have the opportunity to ask questions and make informed decisions about their participation.
Competence and Scope of Practice:

Coaches should practice within their scope of competence, which includes having the necessary education, training, and experience to effectively support clients. Coaches should refer clients to mental health professionals when issues exceed their expertise or require therapeutic intervention beyond coaching.
Boundaries and Dual Relationships:

Coaches should establish and maintain clear boundaries with clients to prevent conflicts of interest and dual relationships. This includes avoiding personal, social, financial, or romantic relationships with clients that could compromise objectivity, professionalism, or the coaching relationship.
Professionalism and Integrity:

Coaches should uphold high standards of professionalism and integrity in their interactions with clients and colleagues. This includes being honest, transparent, and accountable for their actions, maintaining punctuality, and respecting clients' time and resources.
Conflict of Interest:

Coaches should identify and manage potential conflicts of interest that may arise from personal or professional relationships that could influence coaching practices or decisions. Coaches should prioritize clients' best interests and avoid situations where personal gain or bias may compromise ethical standards.

Cultural Sensitivity and Diversity:

Coaches should demonstrate cultural sensitivity and respect for diversity in coaching practice. This involves understanding and valuing clients' cultural backgrounds, beliefs, and values, and adapting coaching approaches to be inclusive and culturally responsive.

Continuous Professional Development:

Coaches should engage in ongoing professional development to stay updated with best practices, ethical guidelines, and industry standards. Continuing education, supervision, peer consultation, and participation in professional associations contribute to ethical competence and growth as a coach.

Ethical Decision-Making:

Coaches should develop ethical decision-making skills to navigate complex situations that may arise in coaching practice. Ethical dilemmas should be approached with careful consideration of ethical principles, consultation with colleagues or supervisors, and adherence to legal and professional guidelines.

By maintaining awareness of these ethical considerations and adhering to professional standards, mental health coaches can uphold the integrity of their practice, promote client well-being, and foster trust and confidence in the coaching relationship. Ethical practice not only safeguards clients but also contributes to the credibility and effectiveness of mental health coaching as a valuable support modality.

Chapter 7: What are the emerging trends and innovations in mental health coaching?

Emerging trends and innovations in mental health coaching reflect advancements in technology, changes in societal attitudes toward mental health, and evolving client needs. Here are some notable trends:

Integration of Technology:

Telehealth and Digital Platforms: The use of telehealth platforms for remote coaching sessions has increased accessibility and convenience for clients. Coaches can conduct sessions via video conferencing, phone calls, or secure messaging platforms, accommodating clients' schedules and preferences.

Mobile Apps and Digital Tools: There is a growing availability of mobile apps and digital tools designed to support mental health coaching. These tools may include mood tracking apps, mindfulness meditation apps, cognitive behavioral therapy (CBT) tools, and virtual coaching platforms that enhance engagement and provide continuous support between sessions.

AI and Machine Learning:

AI-driven tools are being developed to analyze client data, personalize coaching interventions, and provide insights into mental health trends and patterns. Machine learning algorithms can assist coaches in identifying client needs, predicting outcomes, and optimizing coaching strategies based on data analytics.

Focus on Prevention and Well-being:

There is a shift toward preventive mental health coaching, focusing on enhancing resilience, promoting well-being, and preventing mental health challenges before they escalate. Coaches emphasize proactive strategies such as stress management, lifestyle modifications, and building emotional resilience to maintain mental health.

Specialized Coaching Niches:

Mental health coaching is diversifying into specialized niches tailored to specific populations or needs. Examples include coaching for corporate executives, athletes, students, parents, caregivers, and individuals managing chronic illnesses. Specialized coaching niches cater to unique challenges and goals within these demographics.
Holistic Approaches:

Coaches are integrating holistic approaches that address the interconnected aspects of well-being, including physical health, nutrition, sleep, social relationships, and spirituality. Holistic coaching frameworks recognize the importance of lifestyle factors in mental health and aim to optimize overall wellness through comprehensive interventions.
Cultural Competence and Inclusivity:

There is a growing emphasis on cultural competence and inclusivity in mental health coaching. Coaches are increasingly trained to recognize and respect diverse cultural backgrounds, beliefs, and values, ensuring that coaching approaches are relevant and sensitive to clients' cultural identities and experiences.
Evidence-Based Practices:

Mental health coaching is increasingly embracing evidence-based practices validated by research. Coaches are integrating techniques from fields such as cognitive behavioral therapy (CBT), positive psychology, mindfulness-based interventions, and neuroscience-informed approaches to enhance coaching effectiveness and client outcomes.
Collaborative Care Models:

Coaches are collaborating with other healthcare professionals, such as psychologists, psychiatrists, primary care physicians, and wellness practitioners, to provide integrated care. Collaborative care models ensure holistic support for clients, addressing both mental health and physical health needs in coordinated efforts.
Personalized and Adaptive Coaching:

Advances in personalized coaching involve tailoring interventions to individual client preferences, goals, learning styles, and personality traits. Coaches use assessments, client feedback, and ongoing evaluation to adapt coaching strategies and optimize client engagement and outcomes over time. These emerging trends and innovations reflect the dynamic evolution of mental health coaching, aiming to meet the diverse needs of clients, leverage technological advancements, and enhance the accessibility and effectiveness of mental health support services. As the field continues to grow, coaches are positioned to integrate these innovations while upholding ethical standards and promoting positive mental health outcomes for their clients.

Chapter 8: How can mental health coaching promote personal growth, resilience, and emotional intelligence?

Mental health coaching plays a crucial role in promoting personal growth, resilience, and emotional intelligence by providing individuals with personalized support, tools, and strategies to navigate challenges, enhance self-awareness, and develop adaptive skills. Here's how mental health coaching can achieve these goals:

Self-Awareness and Reflection:

Mental health coaches facilitate self-discovery and introspection through reflective exercises, discussions, and feedback. By exploring thoughts, emotions, and behavioral patterns, clients gain deeper insights into their strengths, values, and areas for growth. Increased self-awareness fosters personal growth by empowering clients to make informed decisions and align actions with personal goals and values.
Goal Setting and Achievement:

Coaches collaborate with clients to establish realistic and meaningful goals that promote personal growth and resilience. Goal-setting techniques focus on breaking down objectives into manageable steps, monitoring progress, and celebrating achievements. By setting clear intentions and taking proactive steps toward goals, clients build confidence, motivation, and a sense of accomplishment.
Building Resilience:

Resilience-building strategies in mental health coaching equip clients with skills to adaptively cope with adversity, setbacks, and stressors. Coaches emphasize resilience factors such as problem-solving skills, positive coping mechanisms, social support networks, and fostering a growth mindset. Through resilience training, clients develop the capacity to bounce back from challenges, maintain perspective during difficult times, and navigate transitions with greater ease.
Emotional Regulation and Management:

Coaches teach techniques for emotional regulation and stress management, enhancing clients' ability to identify, understand, and effectively manage their emotions. Mindfulness practices, relaxation techniques, cognitive reframing, and assertiveness training empower clients to respond to emotional triggers constructively, reduce anxiety, and cultivate emotional resilience. Improved emotional intelligence allows clients to navigate relationships, make sound decisions, and maintain emotional well-being.
Enhancing Communication Skills:

Coaching interventions focus on improving interpersonal communication, assertiveness, and conflict resolution skills. Effective communication enhances relationship dynamics, fosters empathy and understanding, and promotes mutual respect. Coaches guide clients in expressing needs, setting boundaries, and cultivating supportive relationships that contribute to emotional well-being and personal growth.
Cognitive Restructuring and Positive Thinking:

Cognitive-behavioral techniques, such as cognitive restructuring and positive psychology interventions, help clients challenge negative thought patterns, overcome self-limiting beliefs, and cultivate a more optimistic outlook. Coaches encourage clients to reframe challenges as opportunities for growth, focus on strengths and achievements, and develop a resilient mindset that fosters perseverance and adaptability.
Integrating Learnings into Daily Life:

Mental health coaching emphasizes the application of insights and skills gained in coaching sessions to real-life situations. Coaches support clients in implementing action plans, practicing new behaviors, and integrating sustainable habits that promote ongoing personal growth and resilience. Regular reflection and adjustment of strategies ensure continued progress and adaptation to changing circumstances.

By fostering self-awareness, empowering goal achievement, building resilience, enhancing emotional intelligence, and promoting effective communication, mental health coaching equips individuals with the tools and mindset to thrive personally and professionally. The supportive relationship between coach and client facilitates transformative growth, empowering clients to navigate life challenges with confidence, resilience, and a sense of purpose.

Chapter 9: What are the potential career paths and opportunities for mental health coaches?

Mental health coaching offers diverse career paths and opportunities across various sectors, driven by increasing awareness of mental health, demand for personalized support services, and integration of coaching into holistic wellness approaches. Here are some potential career paths and opportunities for mental health coaches:

Private Practice:

Many mental health coaches establish private practices, offering individual coaching sessions, group coaching programs, workshops, and retreats focused on mental health and well-being. Private practice allows coaches to specialize in niche areas, such as anxiety management, stress reduction, resilience building, or personal development.
Corporate Wellness Programs:

Coaches collaborate with organizations to design and implement employee wellness programs that incorporate mental health coaching. Corporate wellness initiatives may include stress management workshops, leadership development coaching, mindfulness training, and promoting work-life balance. Coaches help employees enhance resilience, productivity, and job satisfaction.
Healthcare Settings:

Mental health coaches work alongside healthcare professionals in hospitals, clinics, and medical practices to provide complementary support to patients. Coaches assist individuals managing chronic illnesses, recovery from medical procedures, or coping with lifestyle changes by offering emotional support, behavior change strategies, and health education.
Educational Institutions:

Coaches collaborate with schools, colleges, and universities to support students' mental health and personal development. Educational coaching programs focus on stress management, academic performance, career exploration, and enhancing student resilience. Coaches may also work with faculty and staff to promote wellness initiatives.
Community Health Organizations:

Coaches partner with community health centers, non-profit organizations, and social service agencies to deliver mental health coaching to underserved populations. Coaches address social determinants of health, promote health equity, and support individuals facing economic challenges, trauma, or mental health disparities.
Telehealth and Online Coaching Platforms:

With the rise of telehealth and digital platforms, mental health coaches provide virtual coaching services to clients worldwide. Online coaching platforms offer opportunities for coaches to reach a broader audience, deliver personalized coaching sessions, and utilize digital tools for goal tracking, communication, and client engagement.
Wellness Retreats and Workshops:

Coaches organize and facilitate wellness retreats, workshops, and group coaching programs focused on mental health, mindfulness, personal growth, and holistic well-being. Retreats offer immersive experiences that combine coaching sessions with activities such as yoga, meditation, nature walks, and creative therapies.
Consulting and Training:

Experienced mental health coaches may transition into consulting roles, offering expertise to healthcare providers, organizations, and coaching professionals. Consultants advise on program development, best practices in mental health coaching, ethical standards, and integrating coaching into existing services.
Research and Education:

Coaches contribute to mental health research, education, and advocacy by publishing articles, conducting studies, and presenting at conferences. They may teach coaching courses, develop curriculum for coaching certification programs, and mentor aspiring coaches in ethical practice and professional development.
Specialized Coaching Niches:

Coaches specialize in niche areas such as addiction recovery coaching, trauma-informed coaching, health and wellness coaching, executive coaching, career coaching, and life transitions coaching. Specialization allows coaches to tailor services to specific client needs and interests, enhancing expertise and marketability.
These career paths illustrate the versatility and impact of mental health coaching in supporting individuals, organizations, and communities in achieving mental well-being, resilience, and personal growth. Coaches can explore diverse opportunities that align with their interests, expertise, and professional goals within the evolving landscape of mental health and wellness.

Chapter 10: How can individuals find a qualified mental health coach, and what should they look for in a coaching relationship?

Finding a qualified mental health coach involves a thoughtful approach to ensure compatibility, expertise, and ethical standards. Here are steps individuals can take to find a qualified mental health coach and what to look for in a coaching relationship:

Steps to Find a Qualified Mental Health Coach:
Define Your Goals and Needs:

Clarify what you hope to achieve through coaching, whether it's managing stress, enhancing resilience, improving relationships, or achieving personal growth. Understanding your goals will guide the search for a coach with relevant expertise.
Research and Referrals:

Seek recommendations from trusted sources, such as healthcare providers, therapists, friends, or colleagues who have experience with coaching. Online directories, professional associations, and social media platforms may also provide listings of qualified coaches.
Evaluate Qualifications and Experience:

Review the coach's credentials, certifications, and training in mental health coaching or related fields. Look for coaches who have completed accredited coaching programs, hold certifications from reputable coaching organizations (e.g., International Coach Federation), and have experience working with clients facing similar challenges.
Assess Specialization and Approach:

Consider whether the coach specializes in areas relevant to your needs, such as anxiety management, career transitions, mindfulness, or holistic wellness. Understand the coach's coaching approach, techniques used (e.g., cognitive-behavioral coaching, positive psychology), and compatibility with your preferences and values.

Initial Consultation:

Schedule an initial consultation or discovery call with potential coaches to discuss your goals, their coaching approach, fees, scheduling, and client-coach compatibility. Use this opportunity to ask questions about their experience, coaching philosophy, and how they tailor coaching to individual needs.

Ethical Standards and Boundaries:

Inquire about the coach's adherence to ethical guidelines, confidentiality policies, and boundaries in the coaching relationship. A qualified coach should prioritize client confidentiality, maintain professional boundaries, and ensure a safe and supportive environment for coaching sessions.

What to Look for in a Coaching Relationship:

Trust and Rapport:

A strong coaching relationship is built on trust, mutual respect, and open communication. Ensure you feel comfortable sharing personal experiences and challenges with your coach, knowing they will be approached with empathy and confidentiality.

Goal Alignment and Accountability:

A qualified coach collaborates with you to set clear, achievable goals and creates a structured plan to track progress. They should encourage accountability, provide constructive feedback, and celebrate milestones along the coaching journey.

Empathetic Listening and Support:

Effective coaches demonstrate active listening skills, empathy, and non-judgmental support. They should validate your experiences, help clarify perspectives, and provide encouragement during difficult moments.
Customized Approach and Flexibility:

Look for a coach who customizes their approach to your unique needs, preferences, and learning style. They should be adaptable and willing to adjust coaching techniques based on your progress and evolving goals.
Commitment to Continuous Learning:

A qualified coach invests in their professional development, staying informed about best practices, emerging trends, and ethical standards in coaching. They may participate in supervision, peer consultation, and continuing education to enhance their coaching effectiveness.
Outcome-Oriented Results:

Evaluate the effectiveness of coaching by assessing whether you are achieving your desired outcomes, developing new skills, and experiencing positive changes in your life. A successful coaching relationship empowers you to apply insights gained in coaching sessions to real-life situations. Choosing a qualified mental health coach involves careful consideration of credentials, specialization, coaching approach, and compatibility with your personal goals and values. By prioritizing these factors and fostering a collaborative coaching relationship, individuals can benefit from personalized support, growth, and enhanced well-being under the guidance of a skilled mental health coach.

Chapter 11: Definition and scope of mental health coaching

Mental health coaching is a specialized form of coaching focused on supporting individuals in enhancing their mental well-being, resilience, and emotional health. Unlike therapy or counseling, which often delve into past experiences and clinical diagnoses, mental health coaching primarily focuses on the present and future, empowering clients to achieve personal and professional goals related to mental wellness.

The scope of mental health coaching encompasses various aspects of psychological and emotional health, including stress management, anxiety reduction, goal setting, improving self-confidence, and developing coping strategies. Coaches work collaboratively with clients to explore their strengths, values, and aspirations, providing guidance, accountability, and practical tools to navigate challenges and foster positive change.

Key elements of mental health coaching include:

Goal-Oriented Approach: Coaches help clients clarify their goals and aspirations related to mental well-being, establishing actionable steps to achieve them.

Skills Development: Coaching sessions focus on developing skills such as emotional intelligence, resilience, mindfulness, and effective communication to enhance mental health.

Behavioral Change: Coaches support clients in identifying and modifying behaviors that may hinder their well-being, promoting sustainable changes for long-term growth.

Holistic Perspective: Mental health coaching considers the interplay between physical, emotional, and social factors impacting mental well-being, advocating for a holistic approach to health.

Empowerment and Support: Coaches empower clients to take ownership of their mental health journey, offering non-judgmental support, encouragement, and accountability throughout the coaching process.

By integrating evidence-based practices from psychology, neuroscience, and coaching methodologies, mental health coaching aims to cultivate resilience, promote self-awareness, and equip individuals with the tools needed to thrive mentally and emotionally in all aspects of life.

Chapter 12: Historical perspective and evolution of mental health coaching

The historical perspective and evolution of mental health coaching trace back to the late 20th century, emerging as a distinct discipline blending principles of psychology, coaching, and personal development. Here are key milestones in its development:

Origins in Coaching Psychology: Mental health coaching draws from coaching psychology, which evolved in the 1980s and 1990s as an approach focused on enhancing personal effectiveness and well-being through coaching techniques. Initially rooted in sports and executive coaching, the field expanded to encompass mental health domains.

Integration of Positive Psychology: With the rise of positive psychology in the 1990s, mental health coaching embraced a strengths-based approach. Coaches began emphasizing clients' strengths, resilience, and potential for growth rather than solely focusing on pathology or deficits.

Shift from Therapy to Coaching: Mental health coaching distinguishes itself from therapy by emphasizing goal-setting, personal growth, and practical strategies for enhancing mental well-being, rather than clinical treatment of mental disorders. This shift attracted individuals seeking proactive support for improving mental health and life satisfaction.

Emergence of Specialized Training: As demand grew, specialized training programs and certifications for mental health coaching emerged. Organizations such as the International Coach Federation (ICF) began offering credentials specific to coaching in mental health contexts, establishing standards for ethical practice and professional development.

Integration into Healthcare and Wellness: Mental health coaching gained recognition as a valuable complement to traditional healthcare and wellness practices. Coaches collaborate with healthcare providers, employers, and community organizations to promote mental health, stress management, and overall well-being.

Research and Evidence-Based Practices: The field continues to evolve with ongoing research into the effectiveness of coaching interventions for mental health outcomes. Evidence-based practices from fields like cognitive-behavioral therapy (CBT), positive psychology, and neuroscience inform coaching approaches, ensuring relevance and efficacy.

Global Expansion and Diversity: Mental health coaching has expanded globally, adapting to diverse cultural contexts and healthcare systems. Coaches increasingly tailor their approaches to address cultural nuances, societal norms, and individual preferences, promoting inclusivity and accessibility in mental health support.

Today, mental health coaching stands as a dynamic profession bridging psychology and coaching, offering individuals proactive support, skill development, and empowerment to enhance mental well-being and achieve personal growth. Its evolution continues to shape how individuals approach and prioritize mental health in their lives.

Chapter 13: The Role of a Mental Health Coach

The role of a mental health coach encompasses a multifaceted approach aimed at empowering individuals to achieve mental well-being and personal growth through supportive and collaborative coaching relationships. Here are key aspects that define the role of a mental health coach:

Support and Guidance: Mental health coaches provide non-judgmental support and guidance to clients navigating challenges related to mental health, stress management, and emotional well-being. They offer a safe space for clients to explore their thoughts, feelings, and goals.

Goal Setting and Action Planning: Coaches collaborate with clients to identify and clarify their goals related to mental health and personal development. They assist in creating actionable plans, setting realistic milestones, and tracking progress towards achieving desired outcomes.

Strengths-Based Approach: Adopting a strengths-based perspective, coaches help clients leverage their strengths, values, and resources to overcome obstacles and enhance resilience. They focus on empowering clients to build on their existing capabilities and develop new skills.

Skill Development: Mental health coaches facilitate skill development in areas such as mindfulness, emotional intelligence, effective communication, and stress management. They teach practical techniques and strategies that empower clients to cope with challenges and improve their overall well-being.

Accountability and Motivation: Coaches hold clients accountable for taking steps towards their goals, providing encouragement, motivation, and constructive feedback along the way. They help clients stay committed to their action plans and navigate setbacks effectively.

Education and Psychoeducation: Coaches educate clients about mental health concepts, evidence-based practices, and behavioral strategies that promote mental well-being. They may offer psychoeducation on topics such as anxiety management, resilience building, and healthy lifestyle habits.

Collaboration with Healthcare Professionals: In some cases, mental health coaches collaborate with therapists, counselors, and healthcare providers to ensure holistic care for clients. They may refer clients to appropriate professionals when specialized mental health treatment is needed.

Ethical Considerations: Mental health coaches adhere to ethical guidelines, confidentiality standards, and professional boundaries in their practice. They prioritize the well-being and autonomy of clients while promoting a safe and supportive coaching environment.

Continuous Professional Development: Coaches engage in ongoing learning, supervision, and professional development to stay informed about best practices in mental health coaching. They may pursue certifications, attend workshops, and participate in peer consultation to enhance their coaching skills and knowledge.

Overall, the role of a mental health coach is centered on empowering individuals to cultivate resilience, enhance self-awareness, and achieve greater fulfillment in their personal and professional lives through collaborative coaching relationships focused on mental well-being.

Chapter 14: Responsibilities and ethical considerations

The responsibilities of a mental health coach are intertwined with ethical considerations that uphold the integrity and effectiveness of their practice. Here's an overview of the responsibilities and ethical considerations that guide mental health coaches:

Responsibilities:
Client-Centered Approach: Mental health coaches prioritize the needs, goals, and well-being of their clients. They establish a collaborative coaching relationship based on trust, respect, and confidentiality.

Goal Setting and Action Planning: Coaches assist clients in identifying and clarifying their goals related to mental health and personal development. They help clients create actionable plans, set achievable milestones, and track progress over time.

Skill Development and Education: Coaches facilitate the development of skills such as mindfulness, emotional intelligence, stress management, and effective communication. They provide education on mental health topics, evidence-based practices, and behavioral strategies.

Support and Empowerment: Coaches offer empathetic support, encouragement, and motivation to clients as they navigate challenges and work towards their goals. They empower clients to build resilience, leverage strengths, and make positive changes in their lives.

Ethical Guidelines: Coaches adhere to ethical standards set by professional coaching organizations (e.g., International Coach Federation) and relevant laws. They maintain confidentiality, respect client autonomy, and avoid conflicts of interest.

Collaboration and Referrals: Coaches collaborate with other healthcare professionals, therapists, and counselors when appropriate, ensuring holistic care for clients. They may refer clients to specialized services or professionals based on identified needs.

Continuous Professional Development: Coaches engage in ongoing learning, supervision, and professional development to enhance their coaching skills, stay updated on best practices, and maintain competence in the field.

Ethical Considerations:
Confidentiality: Coaches maintain strict confidentiality regarding client information, discussions, and outcomes, unless legally mandated to disclose or with client consent.

Informed Consent: Coaches ensure clients understand the coaching process, goals, roles, and potential outcomes before initiating coaching sessions. They obtain informed consent for coaching services.

Boundaries: Coaches establish and maintain clear boundaries in the coaching relationship to ensure professionalism, clarity, and respect for client autonomy.

Competence: Coaches practice within their scope of competence, skills, and training. They recognize limitations and refer clients to other professionals when issues exceed their expertise.

Conflict of Interest: Coaches avoid conflicts of interest that could compromise the coaching relationship or client welfare. They refrain from dual relationships that may impair objectivity or create undue influence.

Cultural Sensitivity: Coaches respect and integrate cultural differences, values, and beliefs into coaching practices. They strive to understand and accommodate diverse perspectives and backgrounds.

Professional Conduct: Coaches uphold high standards of professional conduct, integrity, and accountability in all interactions with clients, colleagues, and the public.

By adhering to these responsibilities and ethical considerations, mental health coaches maintain a commitment to client well-being, ethical practice, and continuous professional growth, fostering a supportive environment for clients' personal and mental health development.

Chapter 15: Case studies illustrating successful coaching outcomes.

Case studies provide valuable insights into how mental health coaching can effectively support individuals in achieving their goals and improving their well-being. Here are a few hypothetical examples of successful coaching outcomes:

Case Study 1: Stress Management and Work-Life Balance
Client Background: Sarah, a marketing manager in her mid-30s, struggled with chronic stress due to high work demands and balancing family responsibilities.

Coaching Approach: Sarah worked with a mental health coach to identify sources of stress and develop strategies for better work-life balance. The coach used mindfulness techniques and goal-setting exercises to help Sarah prioritize tasks, delegate responsibilities, and set boundaries.

Outcome: Over several months of coaching, Sarah reported reduced stress levels, improved sleep quality, and enhanced coping mechanisms for managing work pressures. She successfully implemented strategies to create more time for family activities and self-care, resulting in a more balanced and fulfilling life.

Case Study 2: Anxiety Management and Emotional Resilience
Client Background: James, a recent college graduate in his early 20s, experienced generalized anxiety and struggled with self-doubt in social situations.

Coaching Approach: James worked with a mental health coach who specialized in anxiety management techniques. The coach utilized cognitive-behavioral coaching (CBC) methods to challenge negative thought patterns, develop relaxation techniques, and enhance self-confidence through gradual exposure exercises.

Outcome: Through consistent coaching sessions, James reported decreased anxiety symptoms, improved self-esteem, and greater confidence in social interactions. He learned practical skills to manage anxious thoughts and developed a proactive mindset for handling stressful situations effectively.

Case Study 3: Personal Growth and Career Transition
Client Background: Emily, a middle-aged professional, felt stuck in her current career and desired a transition into a more fulfilling role aligned with her passions.

Coaching Approach: Emily collaborated with a mental health coach who specialized in career coaching and personal development. The coach conducted assessments to identify Emily's strengths, values, and career aspirations. They created a step-by-step action plan that included networking strategies, skill development opportunities, and interview preparation.

Outcome: With the support of her coach, Emily successfully navigated a career transition, secured a new position in a field that aligned with her interests, and reported increased job satisfaction and personal fulfillment. She credited the coaching process for providing clarity, motivation, and practical guidance throughout her career journey.

Case Study 4: Wellness and Lifestyle Change
Client Background: John, a middle-aged executive, struggled with unhealthy lifestyle habits, including poor diet and lack of exercise, leading to weight gain and low energy levels.

Coaching Approach: John engaged with a mental health coach who specialized in wellness coaching. The coach conducted a comprehensive assessment of John's health behaviors and goals. They collaborated on setting achievable goals for nutrition, physical activity, and stress management. The coach provided ongoing support, accountability, and motivational strategies to help John adopt healthier habits.

Outcome: Over the course of coaching sessions, John made significant lifestyle changes, including improved dietary choices, regular exercise routine, and stress reduction techniques. He experienced weight loss, increased energy levels, and a positive shift in overall well-being. John maintained his new habits independently, attributing his success to the personalized support and guidance provided by his coach.

These case studies illustrate the diverse ways in which mental health coaching can facilitate positive change, empower individuals to overcome challenges, and achieve meaningful personal and professional growth. Each example highlights the collaborative efforts between clients and coaches to navigate obstacles, build resilience, and enhance overall quality of life.

Chapter 16: Foundations of Mental Health: Psychology and Neuroscience

The foundations of mental health coaching draw heavily from both psychology and neuroscience, providing a robust framework for understanding human behavior, emotions, and cognitive processes. Here's an exploration of how psychology and neuroscience contribute to the foundational knowledge of mental health coaching:

Psychology:
Understanding Human Behavior: Psychology offers insights into the complexities of human behavior, including cognitive processes, emotions, motivations, and interpersonal relationships. Coaches leverage psychological theories and models to help clients gain self-awareness, identify patterns of thinking, and understand the underlying factors influencing their mental health.

Applying Behavioral Techniques: Techniques derived from behavioral psychology, such as cognitive-behavioral therapy (CBT), are commonly integrated into coaching practices. Coaches use these techniques to help clients challenge negative thought patterns, modify behaviors, and develop adaptive coping strategies for managing stress, anxiety, and other mental health challenges.

Promoting Positive Psychology: Positive psychology emphasizes strengths, resilience, and well-being. Coaches incorporate positive psychology interventions to cultivate optimism, gratitude, mindfulness, and self-efficacy in clients. These approaches aim to enhance psychological resilience and foster a positive mindset conducive to personal growth and fulfillment.

Developing Emotional Intelligence: Emotional intelligence, a key concept in psychology, involves the ability to perceive, understand, manage, and express emotions effectively. Coaches help clients enhance their emotional intelligence through self-awareness exercises, empathy-building techniques, and strategies for regulating emotions in various life situations.

Neuroscience:
Insights into Brain Function: Neuroscience provides a deeper understanding of brain structure, function, and neurochemical processes underlying emotions, cognition, and behavior. Coaches apply neuroscientific knowledge to explain how habits are formed, stress impacts the brain, and mindfulness practices can induce neuroplasticity and promote mental resilience.

Behavior Change Strategies: Coaches integrate neuroscience findings on behavior change to design personalized interventions that align with clients' neurological profiles and learning styles. Techniques such as neurofeedback, which measures brainwave activity to enhance self-regulation, are used to support clients in achieving desired behavioral outcomes.

Impact of Stress and Trauma: Neuroscience informs coaches about the physiological effects of chronic stress, trauma, and adverse childhood experiences on brain development and mental health. Coaches incorporate trauma-informed approaches and stress management techniques grounded in neuroscience to help clients heal, build resilience, and restore emotional balance.

Neuroplasticity and Growth Mindset: The concept of neuroplasticity underscores the brain's ability to adapt and reorganize in response to learning, experiences, and environmental changes. Coaches promote a growth mindset in clients, emphasizing the potential for neuroplasticity through cognitive exercises, mindfulness practices, and intentional behavioral modifications.

Integration in Coaching Practice:
In mental health coaching, the integration of psychology and neuroscience enhances the effectiveness of interventions tailored to clients' unique needs and goals. Coaches leverage evidence-based practices, psychological assessments, and neuroscientific principles to facilitate personal growth, emotional well-being, and sustainable behavior change. By bridging insights from psychology and neuroscience, mental health coaches provide clients with comprehensive support to navigate challenges, enhance self-awareness, and cultivate resilience in pursuit of optimal mental health and life satisfaction.

Chapter 17: Basics of psychology relevant to coaching

The basics of psychology relevant to coaching provide foundational knowledge that coaches use to understand human behavior, facilitate personal growth, and support clients in achieving their goals. Here are key principles of psychology essential to coaching:

Human Development: Understanding human development across the lifespan helps coaches recognize how experiences and milestones shape individuals' perspectives, behaviors, and goals. Coaches apply developmental psychology concepts to support clients in navigating life transitions, personal growth stages, and identity formation.

Cognitive Processes: Cognitive psychology explores how people perceive, process, and interpret information. Coaches utilize cognitive theories to help clients identify and challenge negative thought patterns, enhance self-awareness, and develop cognitive restructuring techniques for improving problem-solving and decision-making skills.

Behavioral Patterns: Behavioral psychology focuses on observable behaviors, habits, and conditioning processes. Coaches assess behavioral patterns to identify factors contributing to clients' challenges and help them implement behavior modification strategies. Techniques like goal-setting, reinforcement, and habit formation are employed to support sustainable behavior change.

Motivation and Goal Setting: Motivational psychology examines factors influencing human motivation, including intrinsic and extrinsic motivators, goal orientation, and self-determination theory. Coaches utilize motivational interviewing techniques to explore clients' motivations, align goals with values, and foster commitment to goal achievement through incremental progress and accountability.

Emotional Regulation: Emotional psychology emphasizes the importance of emotional awareness, regulation, and expression in promoting mental well-being. Coaches help clients develop emotional intelligence by identifying and managing emotions effectively, enhancing self-regulation skills, and cultivating resilience in coping with stress, anxiety, and interpersonal challenges.

Social and Interpersonal Dynamics: Social psychology explores how individuals perceive, influence, and relate to others within social contexts. Coaches incorporate interpersonal skills development, communication strategies, and relationship-building techniques to enhance clients' social competence, assertiveness, and empathy in personal and professional interactions.

Personality and Individual Differences: Personality psychology examines enduring patterns of thoughts, feelings, and behaviors that shape individuals' personality traits and preferences. Coaches use personality assessments and typologies (e.g., Myers-Briggs Type Indicator, Big Five Personality Traits) to tailor coaching approaches, recognize clients' strengths, and support self-discovery and authenticity.

Stress and Coping Mechanisms: Health psychology explores the impact of stress on mental and physical health, as well as effective coping strategies. Coaches educate clients on stress management techniques, relaxation methods, and resilience-building practices to mitigate stressors, promote self-care, and foster adaptive coping mechanisms.

By applying these fundamental principles of psychology, mental health coaches enhance their understanding of clients' perspectives, facilitate meaningful behavior change, and empower individuals to cultivate resilience, achieve personal growth, and optimize their overall well-being through coaching interventions tailored to individual needs and goals.

Chapter 18: Neuroscience insights into behavior change and mental health.

Neuroscience provides valuable insights into behavior change and mental health by examining how brain structure, function, and neurochemical processes influence thoughts, emotions, and behaviors. Here are key neuroscience insights that inform behavior change and mental health practices:

Neuroplasticity: Neuroscience reveals that the brain is plastic, meaning it can reorganize and adapt throughout life in response to learning, experiences, and environmental stimuli. Mental health coaches leverage neuroplasticity to facilitate behavior change by introducing new habits, reinforcing positive behaviors, and promoting neurocognitive flexibility.

Reward Systems: The brain's reward circuitry, primarily involving neurotransmitters like dopamine, motivates behavior by reinforcing pleasurable experiences and outcomes. Coaches use reward-based strategies to motivate clients, such as setting achievable goals, celebrating milestones, and creating positive associations with desired behaviors.

Stress Response: Neuroscience elucidates the physiological stress response mediated by the hypothalamic-pituitary-adrenal (HPA) axis and its impact on mental health. Coaches educate clients on stress management techniques, such as mindfulness, deep breathing, and progressive muscle relaxation, to regulate stress hormones (e.g., cortisol) and mitigate the adverse effects of chronic stress on brain function and emotional well-being.

Emotional Regulation: The prefrontal cortex, involved in executive functions like decision-making and emotional regulation, plays a crucial role in managing emotions and behaviors. Coaches teach clients cognitive-behavioral techniques and mindfulness practices to enhance prefrontal cortex function, improve emotional self-regulation, and reduce impulsivity in response to stressors and triggers.

Neurotransmitter Balance: Neurotransmitters like serotonin, gamma-aminobutyric acid (GABA), and norepinephrine influence mood, cognition, and behavior. Coaches promote mental health through lifestyle interventions that support neurotransmitter balance, such as nutrition, exercise, sleep hygiene, and relaxation techniques, to optimize brain function and emotional stability.

Learning and Memory: Neuroscience explains how synaptic connections strengthen or weaken based on learning experiences, shaping behavior and habit formation. Coaches utilize principles of neuroeducation to enhance learning retention, apply evidence-based practices, and promote adaptive behaviors through repeated practice, visualization, and positive reinforcement.

Neurological Resilience: Building resilience involves strengthening neural pathways associated with adaptive coping mechanisms and stress resilience. Coaches help clients cultivate resilience through cognitive restructuring, problem-solving skills, and social support networks, fostering neurobiological adaptations that enhance emotional well-being and mental health outcomes.

Mind-Body Connection: Neuroscience underscores the interconnectedness of mental and physical health, highlighting the impact of lifestyle factors (e.g., diet, exercise, sleep) on brain function and emotional regulation. Coaches integrate mind-body interventions, such as yoga, tai chi, and biofeedback, to promote holistic well-being and optimize neurobiological health for sustainable behavior change.

By integrating neuroscience insights into coaching practices, mental health coaches empower clients to understand the neurobiological basis of their behaviors, develop personalized strategies for behavior change, and cultivate resilience, emotional well-being, and overall mental health.

Chapter 19: Integrating evidence-based practices into coaching sessions.

Integrating evidence-based practices into coaching sessions is crucial for ensuring effectiveness, reliability, and ethical standards in mental health coaching. Here's how mental health coaches can incorporate evidence-based practices (EBPs) into their sessions:

1. Understanding Evidence-Based Practices (EBPs)
Definition: EBPs are interventions or techniques supported by rigorous research, demonstrating their effectiveness in improving specific outcomes related to mental health.

Examples: Cognitive Behavioral Therapy (CBT), mindfulness-based interventions, motivational interviewing, and solution-focused brief therapy are examples of EBPs commonly integrated into coaching sessions.

2. Steps to Integrate EBPs into Coaching
Assessment and Client-Centered Approach

Assessment: Conduct thorough assessments to understand clients' needs, strengths, and challenges. Use validated tools and measures to gather baseline data and monitor progress.

Collaborative Goal Setting: Collaborate with clients to establish clear, achievable goals aligned with their values and preferences. Ensure goals are specific, measurable, attainable, relevant, and time-bound (SMART).

Application of EBPs
Tailoring Interventions: Select EBPs based on client characteristics, preferences, and the presenting issue. Customize interventions to fit individual needs and circumstances.

Skill Building: Teach clients practical skills derived from EBPs, such as relaxation techniques, cognitive restructuring, problem-solving strategies, and emotion regulation exercises.

Monitoring and Feedback
Progress Monitoring: Regularly assess client progress towards goals using objective measures and client-reported outcomes. Adjust interventions as needed based on feedback and progress indicators.

Feedback: Encourage open communication to gather client feedback on the effectiveness and relevance of interventions. Use feedback to refine coaching strategies and enhance engagement.

3. Ethics and Professional Standards
Ethical Considerations: Adhere to ethical guidelines and standards of practice in mental health coaching. Maintain confidentiality, respect client autonomy, and obtain informed consent for interventions.

Continuing Education: Stay updated on the latest research and developments in mental health interventions. Participate in continuing education programs to enhance skills and integrate new EBPs into practice.

4. Documentation and Evaluation
Documentation: Keep accurate records of coaching sessions, including goals, interventions used, client progress, and outcomes. Document any modifications to interventions and reasons for changes.

Outcome Evaluation: Evaluate the effectiveness of EBPs by assessing changes in client outcomes, such as symptom reduction, improved functioning, and enhanced well-being. Use outcome data to inform future coaching strategies and interventions.

Benefits of Integrating EBPs
Effectiveness: EBPs have a strong evidence base supporting their effectiveness in addressing specific mental health concerns and promoting positive outcomes.

Client Satisfaction: Clients are more likely to benefit from structured, evidence-based interventions tailored to their needs and preferences.

Professional Credibility: Demonstrating proficiency in integrating EBPs enhances professional credibility and fosters trust with clients, colleagues, and stakeholders.

By integrating evidence-based practices into coaching sessions, mental health coaches can enhance the quality of care, facilitate meaningful client outcomes, and contribute to the advancement of ethical and effective practices in mental health coaching.

Chapter 20: Techniques and Approaches in Mental Health Coaching

Techniques and approaches in mental health coaching encompass a variety of methods aimed at promoting well-being, facilitating personal growth, and addressing mental health challenges. Here's an overview of key techniques and approaches commonly used in mental health coaching:

1. Cognitive Behavioral Coaching (CBC)
Definition: CBC integrates principles from cognitive behavioral therapy (CBT) into coaching sessions. It focuses on identifying and challenging negative thought patterns (cognitive restructuring) and modifying behaviors to promote positive change.

Application: Coaches help clients recognize cognitive distortions, reframe negative thoughts, set realistic goals, and implement behavioral strategies to achieve desired outcomes.

2. Positive Psychology Interventions
Focus: Positive psychology emphasizes strengths, virtues, and factors that contribute to psychological well-being and resilience.

Approaches: Coaches use interventions such as gratitude exercises, strengths assessments (e.g., VIA Character Strengths), and goal-setting aligned with clients' values to enhance positive emotions, engagement, and meaning in life.

3. Mindfulness-Based Approaches
Techniques: Mindfulness practices involve cultivating present-moment awareness, non-judgmental acceptance, and compassion toward oneself and others.

Benefits: Coaches teach mindfulness techniques, such as meditation, deep breathing, and body scan exercises, to promote stress reduction, emotional regulation, and overall mental clarity.

4. Solution-Focused Brief Therapy (SFBT)
Focus: SFBT emphasizes identifying solutions and building on clients' strengths rather than dwelling on problems.

Techniques: Coaches use scaling questions, miracle question, and exception-finding to help clients envision and work towards their preferred futures. SFBT is goal-oriented and emphasizes small, achievable steps.

5. Motivational Interviewing (MI)
Purpose: MI helps clients explore ambivalence and increase motivation for behavior change.

Skills: Coaches use open-ended questions, reflective listening, affirmations, and summaries to elicit clients' intrinsic motivations, enhance commitment to change, and resolve ambivalence towards adopting healthier behaviors.

6. Integrative and Holistic Approaches

Holistic Focus: Coaches consider clients' physical, emotional, social, and spiritual dimensions of well-being.

Approaches: Integrative coaching may incorporate elements from various therapeutic modalities, lifestyle medicine, nutrition counseling, and alternative therapies (e.g., yoga, art therapy) to support overall health and wellness.

7. Strength-Based Approaches

Principles: Strength-based coaching emphasizes identifying and leveraging clients' strengths, resources, and past successes.

Application: Coaches use appreciative inquiry, goal-setting based on strengths, and positive feedback to empower clients, build resilience, and foster self-efficacy in achieving personal and professional goals.

8. Behavioral Activation

Purpose: Behavioral activation aims to increase engagement in rewarding activities and behaviors that align with clients' values.

Strategies: Coaches help clients identify pleasurable and meaningful activities, set behavioral goals, and overcome barriers to activity engagement. This approach is particularly effective in treating depression and mood disorders.

9. Narrative and Expressive Therapies

Approaches: Coaches may integrate narrative techniques and expressive arts therapies (e.g., journaling, storytelling, creative writing, visual arts) to explore personal narratives, facilitate emotional expression, and promote insight and healing.
Integration and Flexibility
Effective mental health coaching involves integrating these techniques and approaches based on clients' preferences, needs, cultural considerations, and the coach's expertise. Coaches tailor interventions to support clients in achieving their goals, enhancing resilience, and fostering sustainable behavior change and well-being.

Chapter 21: Cognitive Behavioral Coaching (CBC) techniques

Cognitive Behavioral Coaching (CBC) integrates principles from cognitive behavioral therapy (CBT) into coaching practices to help clients address unhelpful thought patterns, behaviors, and emotions. Here are key CBC techniques commonly used in mental health coaching:

Identifying Cognitive Distortions:

Description: CBC helps clients recognize and challenge cognitive distortions or irrational thoughts that contribute to negative emotions and behaviors.

Techniques: Coaches use methods such as thought records, where clients document their thoughts, emotions, and the associated situations to identify patterns of cognitive distortions like black-and-white thinking, catastrophizing, and overgeneralization.
Cognitive Restructuring:

Description: CBC aims to reframe negative or distorted thinking patterns into more balanced and realistic perspectives.
Techniques: Coaches guide clients through cognitive restructuring exercises, helping them examine evidence for and against their negative thoughts, develop alternative interpretations, and cultivate more adaptive responses.
Behavioral Activation:

Description: CBC encourages clients to engage in activities that promote positive emotions and behavior change, particularly useful in addressing depression and low motivation.
Techniques: Coaches collaboratively set behavioral goals with clients, break them down into manageable steps, and use activity scheduling to increase engagement in rewarding and meaningful activities that align with clients' values.
Goal Setting and Action Planning:

Description: CBC focuses on setting clear, specific, and achievable goals that promote personal growth and desired behavioral changes.
Techniques: Coaches assist clients in setting SMART goals (Specific, Measurable, Achievable, Relevant, Time-bound), develop action plans with concrete steps, and monitor progress towards goal attainment. They may also explore potential obstacles and develop strategies to overcome them.
Problem-Solving Skills:

Description: CBC equips clients with effective problem-solving techniques to manage challenges and improve decision-making skills.

Techniques: Coaches guide clients through structured problem-solving steps, including defining the problem, brainstorming solutions, evaluating options, implementing a plan, and reviewing outcomes. This approach fosters resilience and empowers clients to tackle difficulties proactively.

Relaxation and Stress Management:

Description: CBC incorporates relaxation techniques to reduce stress, manage anxiety, and promote emotional well-being.

Techniques: Coaches teach clients relaxation methods such as deep breathing, progressive muscle relaxation, guided imagery, and mindfulness exercises. These techniques help clients cultivate relaxation responses, improve self-regulation, and enhance overall coping skills.

Assertiveness Training:

Description: CBC focuses on developing assertiveness skills to improve communication, set boundaries, and assert personal needs effectively.

Techniques: Coaches use role-playing, assertiveness scripts, and behavioral rehearsal to help clients practice assertive communication, express their thoughts and feelings confidently, and negotiate relationships and situations assertively.

By integrating these cognitive behavioral coaching techniques into sessions, coaches empower clients to challenge unproductive thoughts, modify behaviors, enhance emotional regulation, and achieve meaningful personal growth and well-being goals. These evidence-based strategies support clients in developing adaptive coping mechanisms and sustaining positive changes in their lives.

Chapter 22: Positive Psychology interventions

Positive Psychology interventions (PPIs) are techniques and practices designed to enhance well-being, promote positive emotions, and foster personal growth. These interventions focus on leveraging individuals' strengths, cultivating positive experiences, and improving overall life satisfaction. Here are several key Positive Psychology interventions commonly used in coaching and therapeutic settings:

Gratitude Exercises:

Description: Gratitude interventions involve cultivating appreciation for positive aspects of life, fostering optimism, and enhancing emotional resilience.

Techniques: Coaches guide clients in keeping a gratitude journal, where they regularly write down things they are grateful for. This practice promotes positive emotions, shifts focus from negativity, and enhances overall well-being.
Strengths Assessment (VIA Character Strengths):

Description: Strengths-based interventions focus on identifying and utilizing personal strengths to promote self-awareness, growth, and achievement.
Techniques: Coaches use tools like the VIA Character Strengths assessment to help clients identify their core strengths and integrate them into daily life and goal-setting. This approach enhances self-efficacy, improves performance, and fosters a sense of fulfillment.
Positive Affirmations:

Description: Affirmations aim to reframe negative self-talk, enhance self-esteem, and promote a positive self-concept.
Techniques: Coaches assist clients in creating and using personalized positive affirmations that reinforce desired behaviors, beliefs, and attitudes. Regular practice helps shift mindset towards optimism and resilience.
Savoring Practices:

Description: Savoring interventions encourage individuals to fully engage in and appreciate positive experiences, enhancing enjoyment and mindfulness.
Techniques: Coaches guide clients in savoring moments by focusing on sensory details, emotions, and meanings associated with pleasurable experiences. This practice increases gratitude, reduces stress, and promotes present-moment awareness.
Mindfulness-Based Interventions:

Description: Mindfulness interventions cultivate non-judgmental awareness of thoughts, emotions, and sensations, promoting mental clarity and emotional regulation.
Techniques: Coaches teach mindfulness practices such as meditation, mindful breathing, body scan exercises, and mindful movement. These techniques enhance self-awareness, reduce stress, and improve overall psychological well-being.
Goal-Setting and Achievement:

Description: Goal-oriented interventions help individuals set meaningful, achievable goals aligned with personal values and strengths.
Techniques: Coaches assist clients in setting SMART goals (Specific, Measurable, Achievable, Relevant, Time-bound), breaking them down into actionable steps, and providing support and accountability. Goal achievement enhances self-confidence, motivation, and life satisfaction.
Acts of Kindness:

Description: Kindness interventions involve performing altruistic acts to cultivate positive emotions, increase social connections, and enhance well-being.
Techniques: Coaches encourage clients to engage in acts of kindness towards others, such as volunteering, helping someone in need, or expressing gratitude. These actions promote empathy, strengthen relationships, and contribute to a sense of purpose and fulfillment.
Positive Psychology interventions are evidence-based approaches that support individuals in building resilience, enhancing psychological strengths, and fostering a positive outlook on life. By integrating these interventions into coaching practices, coaches empower clients to cultivate happiness, achieve personal growth, and thrive in various aspects of their lives.

Chapter 23: Mindfulness-based approaches and their efficacy

Mindfulness-based approaches are therapeutic techniques rooted in mindfulness meditation practices, aimed at enhancing awareness, acceptance, and present-moment focus. These approaches have shown efficacy in various contexts, including mental health coaching, by promoting emotional regulation, stress reduction, and overall well-being. Here's an overview of mindfulness-based approaches and their effectiveness:

What are Mindfulness-Based Approaches?

Mindfulness involves intentionally paying attention to present-moment experiences with openness, curiosity, and acceptance. Mindfulness-based approaches integrate mindfulness practices into therapeutic interventions to cultivate mental clarity, emotional resilience, and psychological well-being.

Techniques and Practices:
Mindfulness Meditation:

Description: Involves focusing attention on the breath, bodily sensations, thoughts, and emotions without judgment. Practicing mindfulness meditation strengthens attentional control and cultivates a non-reactive awareness of internal and external experiences.
Body Scan:

Description: A guided practice where individuals systematically focus attention on different parts of the body, observing sensations and promoting relaxation. Body scan exercises enhance body awareness and reduce physical tension.
Mindful Breathing:

Description: Involves focusing attention on the sensations of breathing, such as the rise and fall of the abdomen or the flow of air through the nostrils. Mindful breathing calms the mind, regulates emotions, and promotes present-moment awareness.
Mindful Movement (Yoga, Tai Chi):

Description: Integrates mindfulness with physical movement to enhance body awareness, balance, and relaxation. Mindful movement practices improve flexibility, reduce stress, and promote overall physical and mental well-being.
Efficacy in Mental Health Coaching:
Stress Reduction:

Mindfulness-based stress reduction (MBSR) techniques, including mindful breathing and body scan exercises, help individuals manage stress by promoting relaxation responses and reducing physiological arousal.
Emotional Regulation:

Mindfulness practices enhance emotional awareness and regulation by teaching individuals to observe and accept their emotions without reacting impulsively. This skill improves self-control, resilience, and adaptive coping strategies.
Cognitive Flexibility:

Practicing mindfulness cultivates cognitive flexibility by reducing rumination and enhancing the ability to shift attention away from negative thoughts. This improves problem-solving skills and promotes a more balanced perspective.
Enhanced Well-Being:

Regular mindfulness practice is associated with increased life satisfaction, positive mood, and overall psychological well-being. It fosters a sense of presence, gratitude, and appreciation for everyday experiences.
Integration in Coaching Sessions:
In mental health coaching, mindfulness-based approaches are integrated to help clients:

Develop self-awareness and insight into their thoughts, emotions, and behaviors.
Cultivate compassion towards oneself and others.
Improve focus, concentration, and productivity.
Enhance interpersonal relationships and communication skills.
Conclusion:

Mindfulness-based approaches are valuable tools in mental health coaching, offering clients practical techniques to manage stress, regulate emotions, and foster resilience. By incorporating these practices into coaching sessions, coaches empower individuals to cultivate a mindful way of living that supports overall well-being and personal growth.

Chapter 24: Addressing Specific Mental Health Challenges

Addressing specific mental health challenges through coaching involves tailoring approaches to help clients manage and overcome issues such as anxiety, depression, and substance abuse. Here's how mental health coaching can effectively address these challenges:

Anxiety and Stress Management:
Identification and Awareness:

Coaches help clients identify triggers and symptoms of anxiety or stress, fostering awareness of how these emotions manifest in their lives.
Cognitive Restructuring:

Utilizing cognitive behavioral techniques, coaches assist clients in challenging and reframing negative thought patterns that contribute to anxiety. This helps clients develop more adaptive responses to stressful situations.
Mindfulness and Relaxation Techniques:

Introducing mindfulness practices and relaxation exercises (e.g., deep breathing, progressive muscle relaxation) helps clients reduce physiological arousal, promote calmness, and enhance stress resilience.
Behavioral Strategies:

Coaches collaborate with clients to implement behavioral changes that alleviate anxiety, such as time management techniques, setting boundaries, and gradual exposure to anxiety-provoking situations.
Goal-Setting and Action Plans:

Setting specific goals related to anxiety management helps clients focus on achievable steps towards reducing anxiety symptoms. Coaches provide support and accountability to maintain progress.
Depression and Mood Disorders:
Understanding Symptoms:

Coaches assist clients in recognizing signs and symptoms of depression, promoting self-awareness and early intervention.
Activity Scheduling and Behavioral Activation:

Encouraging clients to engage in pleasurable and meaningful activities improves mood and motivation. Coaches help clients create structured routines and schedules to increase activity levels.
Cognitive Behavioral Techniques:

Similar to anxiety management, coaches employ cognitive restructuring to challenge negative thoughts and beliefs associated with depression, fostering a more positive outlook.
Social Support and Connection:

Facilitating discussions on building and maintaining supportive relationships helps clients combat feelings of isolation and loneliness, which are common in depression.
Monitoring Progress and Adjusting Strategies:

Regularly assessing client progress and adjusting coaching strategies as needed ensures ongoing support and effectiveness in managing depression symptoms.
Addiction Recovery and Substance Abuse Coaching:
Education and Awareness:

Providing information about addiction, its effects, and available resources helps clients understand their condition and the recovery process.
Motivational Interviewing:

Coaches use motivational interviewing techniques to explore client readiness for change, enhance motivation, and support commitment to recovery goals.
Relapse Prevention Strategies:

Collaboratively developing relapse prevention plans and coping strategies equips clients with skills to manage triggers, cravings, and high-risk situations.
Support Networks:

Encouraging involvement in support groups, therapy, and community resources builds a network of support essential for sustained recovery.
Holistic Approach:

Integrating holistic practices such as mindfulness, stress management, and lifestyle changes supports overall well-being and reduces the likelihood of relapse.
By addressing specific mental health challenges through tailored coaching approaches, coaches empower clients to develop resilience, enhance coping skills, and achieve sustainable improvements in their mental health and overall quality of life.

Chapter 25: Anxiety and stress management

Anxiety and stress management are crucial aspects of mental health coaching, aimed at helping individuals effectively cope with and reduce the impact of anxiety-provoking situations. Here's how mental health coaching can address anxiety and stress management:

Understanding Anxiety and Stress:
Education and Awareness:

Coaches provide psychoeducation about anxiety, its physiological and psychological effects, and common triggers. This helps clients understand their symptoms and normalize their experiences.
Identifying Triggers and Patterns:

Through dialogue and self-reflection, coaches assist clients in identifying specific triggers and patterns that contribute to their anxiety or stress responses.
Cognitive Behavioral Techniques:
Cognitive Restructuring:

Coaches help clients recognize and challenge negative thought patterns and cognitive distortions that amplify anxiety. By reframing thoughts, clients can develop more balanced and realistic perspectives.
Mindfulness-Based Approaches:

Introducing mindfulness practices, such as mindful breathing or body scan exercises, helps clients cultivate present-moment awareness and reduce anxiety by grounding themselves in the here and now.
Behavioral Strategies:
Stress Management Techniques:

Coaches teach stress reduction techniques like deep breathing, progressive muscle relaxation, or guided imagery. These techniques help clients lower physiological arousal and promote relaxation.
Exposure and Response Prevention (ERP):

Gradual exposure to anxiety-provoking situations, coupled with learning adaptive coping responses, helps clients build resilience and reduce fear associated with triggers.
Lifestyle and Self-Care:
Healthy Habits:

Encouraging clients to maintain a balanced lifestyle with regular exercise, adequate sleep, and nutritious eating habits supports overall well-being and reduces susceptibility to stress.
Self-Care Practices:

Promoting self-care activities such as hobbies, relaxation techniques, and time management strategies helps clients prioritize their mental health and build resilience against stressors.
Goal-Setting and Action Plans:
Setting SMART Goals:

Collaborating with clients to set Specific, Measurable, Achievable, Relevant, and Time-bound goals related to anxiety management empowers them to take actionable steps towards improvement.
Monitoring Progress:

Regularly reviewing goals and monitoring progress helps clients stay motivated and allows coaches to adjust strategies as needed to ensure continued growth and success in anxiety management.
Support and Accountability:
Building Support Networks:

Encouraging clients to cultivate supportive relationships and seek professional support when needed strengthens their resilience and provides additional resources for managing anxiety.
Accountability and Follow-Up:

Providing ongoing support and accountability helps clients maintain momentum in their anxiety management efforts, celebrate achievements, and navigate setbacks effectively.

By integrating these strategies and techniques into coaching sessions, mental health coaches empower clients to develop personalized coping mechanisms, enhance their resilience, and achieve greater emotional well-being in the face of anxiety and stress.

Chapter 26: Depression and mood disorders

Depression and mood disorders are complex mental health conditions that mental health coaching can effectively address. Here's how coaching approaches can help individuals manage and alleviate symptoms associated with depression:

Understanding Depression and Mood Disorders:
Education and Awareness:

Coaches provide information about depression, its symptoms, causes, and available treatment options. This helps clients understand their condition and reduces stigma.
Assessment and Goal Setting:

Collaboratively setting goals related to mood improvement, daily functioning, and overall well-being provides clients with a clear direction and motivation for change.
Cognitive Behavioral Techniques:
Cognitive Restructuring:

Coaches assist clients in identifying and challenging negative thought patterns and cognitive distortions that contribute to feelings of hopelessness and low mood.
Behavioral Activation:

Encouraging clients to engage in pleasurable and meaningful activities helps increase positive reinforcement and motivation, combating the tendency to withdraw and isolate.
Supportive Strategies:
Social Support and Connection:

Facilitating discussions on building and maintaining supportive relationships helps clients combat feelings of loneliness and enhances their sense of belonging.
Mindfulness and Relaxation Techniques:

Introducing mindfulness practices, relaxation exercises, and stress management techniques helps clients reduce physiological arousal and improve emotional regulation.
Holistic Approach:
Lifestyle Modifications:

Promoting healthy habits such as regular exercise, balanced nutrition, adequate sleep, and stress reduction techniques supports overall well-being and mood stability.

Self-Care Practices:

Encouraging self-care activities such as hobbies, relaxation techniques, and mindfulness practices empowers clients to prioritize their mental health and emotional well-being.
Monitoring Progress and Adjusting Strategies:
Regular Check-Ins:

Monitoring client progress and adjusting coaching strategies as needed ensures that clients receive personalized support and encouragement throughout their journey.
Coping Skills Development:

Teaching coping skills such as problem-solving, emotion regulation, and resilience-building techniques equips clients with tools to manage depressive symptoms effectively.
Collaboration with Other Professionals:
Referrals and Coordination:
Coordinating with therapists, psychiatrists, or other healthcare professionals ensures comprehensive care and supports clients in accessing specialized treatment when necessary.
Empowerment and Resilience Building:
Strengths-Based Approach:

Focusing on clients' strengths, resources, and past successes fosters resilience and enhances their ability to navigate challenges associated with depression.
Goal Achievement and Celebrations:

Celebrating client achievements and milestones reinforces progress, boosts self-esteem, and encourages continued engagement in the coaching process.

By integrating these strategies into coaching sessions, mental health coaches empower clients to develop personalized strategies for managing depression, improving mood stability, and enhancing overall quality of life.

Chapter 27: Addiction recovery and substance abuse coaching

Addiction recovery and substance abuse coaching are specialized areas where mental health coaching can play a significant role in supporting individuals through their recovery journey. Here's how coaching approaches can effectively address addiction and substance abuse:

Understanding Addiction and Substance Abuse:
Education and Awareness:

Coaches provide information about addiction, its neurobiological basis, common substances of abuse, and the cycle of addiction. This helps clients understand the impact of substance use on their lives.
Assessment and Goal Setting:

Collaboratively setting goals related to sobriety, health improvement, and life skills development provides clients with direction and motivation for change.
Motivational Interviewing:
Exploring Readiness for Change:

Using motivational interviewing techniques, coaches help clients explore their ambivalence about change, enhance intrinsic motivation, and strengthen commitment to recovery goals.
Goal-Oriented Action Plans:

Developing action plans that outline specific steps, milestones, and strategies for achieving sobriety and maintaining recovery reinforces commitment and provides a structured approach to change.
Relapse Prevention Strategies:
Identifying Triggers and High-Risk Situations:

Coaches assist clients in identifying triggers, cravings, and high-risk situations that may lead to relapse. Developing strategies to manage triggers and cope with cravings reduces the likelihood of relapse.
Coping Skills Development:

Teaching coping skills such as stress management, emotion regulation, and problem-solving equips clients with tools to navigate challenges without resorting to substance use.
Supportive Strategies:
Building Support Networks:

Encouraging clients to engage in peer support groups, 12-step programs, and community resources fosters a sense of belonging and provides ongoing support in recovery.
Family and Social Support:

Involving family members and loved ones in the recovery process, when appropriate, enhances communication, strengthens relationships, and promotes a supportive environment for sustained recovery.
Holistic Approach:
Health and Wellness Promotion:

Promoting holistic wellness practices such as regular exercise, balanced nutrition, adequate sleep, and mindfulness techniques supports physical and emotional well-being during recovery.
Personal Growth and Development:

Encouraging clients to pursue personal interests, hobbies, and vocational or educational goals promotes a sense of purpose and fulfillment beyond substance use.
Accountability and Monitoring:
Regular Progress Checks:

Monitoring client progress through regular check-ins, assessments of goals achieved, and adjustments to action plans ensures ongoing support and accountability in the recovery process.
Celebrating Milestones:

Recognizing and celebrating client achievements, whether small or significant, reinforces progress, boosts self-esteem, and motivates continued commitment to sobriety.

Collaboration with Treatment Providers:

Referrals and Coordination:

Coordinating with addiction counselors, medical professionals, and other treatment providers ensures comprehensive care and supports clients in accessing specialized services as needed.

By integrating these strategies into coaching sessions, mental health coaches empower clients to build resilience, develop coping skills, and achieve sustainable recovery from addiction and substance abuse. Coaching provides personalized support and guidance that complements formal treatment, enhances motivation, and promotes long-term sobriety and well-being.

Chapter 28: Coaching for Personal Growth and Resilience

Coaching for personal growth and resilience is an integral part of mental health coaching, aimed at helping individuals enhance their well-being, achieve their goals, and navigate life's challenges with greater strength and adaptability. Here's how mental health coaching can foster personal growth and resilience:

Understanding Personal Growth and Resilience:
Education and Awareness:

Coaches provide information on the concepts of personal growth and resilience, explaining their importance for mental health and overall well-being.
Self-Assessment and Goal Setting:

Helping clients assess their current levels of resilience and areas for growth, and collaboratively setting goals that align with their values and aspirations.
Building Resilience:
Identifying Strengths and Resources:

Coaches assist clients in identifying their inherent strengths, past successes, and available resources that can support resilience-building efforts.
Developing Coping Strategies:

Teaching effective coping strategies for managing stress, adversity, and setbacks, such as problem-solving, emotional regulation, and cognitive reframing.
Enhancing Emotional Intelligence:
Self-Awareness:

Encouraging clients to develop greater self-awareness by reflecting on their emotions, thoughts, and behaviors, and understanding how these impact their interactions and decisions.

Emotional Regulation:

Teaching techniques for managing emotions, such as mindfulness, deep breathing, and cognitive restructuring, to enhance emotional stability and reduce reactivity.
Goal-Setting and Achievement:
SMART Goals:

Collaborating with clients to set Specific, Measurable, Achievable, Relevant, and Time-bound goals that provide clear direction and motivation for personal growth.
Action Planning:

Developing detailed action plans that outline the steps needed to achieve goals, including identifying potential obstacles and strategies for overcoming them.
Fostering Growth Mindset:
Embracing Challenges:

Encouraging clients to view challenges and setbacks as opportunities for learning and growth, fostering a growth mindset that promotes resilience and perseverance.
Celebrating Progress:

Recognizing and celebrating incremental progress and achievements, reinforcing positive behaviors and maintaining motivation.
Enhancing Interpersonal Skills:
Communication Skills:

Teaching effective communication techniques, such as active listening, assertiveness, and empathy, to improve relationships and social support networks.
Conflict Resolution:

Helping clients develop skills for resolving conflicts constructively, fostering healthier relationships and reducing stress from interpersonal tensions.
Promoting Well-Being:
Self-Care Practices:

Encouraging clients to prioritize self-care through activities that promote physical, emotional, and mental well-being, such as exercise, hobbies, and relaxation techniques.
Mindfulness and Relaxation:

Introducing mindfulness practices and relaxation techniques that help clients stay present, reduce stress, and enhance overall well-being.
Overcoming Limiting Beliefs:
Identifying Limiting Beliefs:

Assisting clients in identifying and challenging limiting beliefs that hinder personal growth and resilience, promoting more empowering and positive self-beliefs.
Building Confidence:

Encouraging clients to take on new challenges and step outside their comfort zones, building confidence and reinforcing their ability to handle adversity.
Support and Accountability:
Regular Check-Ins:

Providing ongoing support and accountability through regular coaching sessions, helping clients stay on track with their goals and adjust strategies as needed.
Encouragement and Motivation:

Offering encouragement, motivation, and constructive feedback to help clients maintain momentum and stay committed to their personal growth journey.

By integrating these strategies into coaching sessions, mental health coaches empower clients to develop greater resilience, achieve their personal goals, and enhance their overall quality of life. Coaching for personal growth and resilience provides a structured and supportive environment where clients can explore their potential, overcome challenges, and thrive.

Chapter 29: Building Resilience Through Coaching: Goal-Setting and Achievement in Mental Health Contexts

Understanding Resilience in Mental Health
Definition and Importance:

Resilience is the ability to adapt positively in the face of adversity, stress, or trauma. It is a critical component of mental health and overall well-being.
Resilience helps individuals cope with life's challenges, recover from setbacks, and thrive despite difficulties.
Factors Influencing Resilience:

Personal traits such as optimism, self-efficacy, and emotional regulation.
External factors like social support, access to resources, and a safe environment.
Role of Coaching in Building Resilience:

Coaches provide guidance, support, and strategies to help clients develop resilience.
Coaching fosters a growth mindset, encouraging clients to view challenges as opportunities for growth.
Goal-Setting in Mental Health Contexts
SMART Goals:

Specific: Clearly defined objectives that outline exactly what needs to be achieved.

Measurable: Criteria to track progress and determine when the goal is met.
Achievable: Realistic goals that are attainable given the client's current situation and resources.
Relevant: Goals that align with the client's values, needs, and long-term objectives.
Time-bound: Setting a clear deadline for goal achievement to maintain focus and motivation.
Importance of Goal-Setting:

Provides direction and purpose, helping clients focus their efforts.
Enhances motivation and commitment to personal growth and resilience-building activities.
Offers a sense of accomplishment and progress, boosting self-esteem and confidence.
Techniques for Effective Goal-Setting
Collaborative Goal-Setting:

Working with clients to identify their goals ensures that the objectives are meaningful and relevant.
Collaborative goal-setting enhances client buy-in and increases the likelihood of goal attainment.
Breaking Down Goals:

Dividing larger goals into smaller, manageable steps makes them less overwhelming and more achievable.
Smaller milestones provide frequent opportunities for success and motivation.
Visualizing Success:

Encouraging clients to visualize the successful achievement of their goals can increase motivation and create a positive mindset.
Visualization techniques can also help clients identify potential obstacles and plan strategies to overcome them.

Strategies for Achieving Goals in Mental Health Contexts
Action Planning:

Developing a detailed action plan that outlines specific steps, resources needed, and timelines for achieving goals.
Action plans provide a roadmap for clients, helping them stay organized and focused.
Overcoming Obstacles:

Identifying potential challenges and barriers to goal achievement allows clients to prepare and develop contingency plans.
Coaches can help clients reframe obstacles as learning opportunities and sources of growth.
Monitoring Progress:

Regularly reviewing progress towards goals helps clients stay accountable and make necessary adjustments.
Celebrating milestones and successes reinforces positive behaviors and maintains motivation.
Adaptive Strategies:

Encouraging flexibility in goal pursuit allows clients to adapt to changing circumstances and maintain progress.
Coaches can help clients revise goals and action plans as needed to ensure continued relevance and achievability.
Enhancing Resilience Through Coaching
Building Self-Efficacy:

Helping clients build confidence in their abilities to achieve their goals and handle challenges.
Providing positive reinforcement, feedback, and encouragement to strengthen self-efficacy.
Strengthening Coping Skills:

Teaching effective coping strategies such as problem-solving, stress management, and emotional regulation.
Coaches can provide tools and techniques to help clients manage stress and adversity constructively.
Developing a Support Network:

Encouraging clients to build and maintain supportive relationships that provide emotional and practical support.
Coaches can help clients identify and connect with social support resources.
Promoting Self-Care:

Emphasizing the importance of self-care practices in maintaining mental health and resilience.
Coaches can guide clients in developing personalized self-care routines that support their well-being.
Conclusion
Building resilience through coaching involves setting and achieving meaningful goals that enhance clients' ability to adapt to life's challenges. By providing support, strategies, and encouragement, coaches empower clients to develop resilience, achieve personal growth, and improve their overall mental health. This chapter highlights the importance of goal-setting and offers practical techniques for fostering resilience in coaching contexts.

Chapter 30: Enhancing Emotional Intelligence and Self-Awareness

Understanding Emotional Intelligence (EI)
Definition and Components of EI:

Self-Awareness: Recognizing and understanding one's own emotions, strengths, weaknesses, values, and drivers.
Self-Regulation: Managing one's emotions, impulses, and behaviors effectively in different situations.
Motivation: Harnessing emotions to pursue goals with energy and persistence.
Empathy: Recognizing, understanding, and considering other people's emotions.
Social Skills: Managing relationships to move people in desired directions.
Importance of EI in Mental Health Coaching:

EI contributes to better mental health, improved relationships, and effective coping strategies.
Enhancing EI helps clients navigate social complexities, manage stress, and make informed decisions.
Techniques for Enhancing Emotional Intelligence
Self-Awareness Development:

Reflective Practices: Encouraging journaling, mindfulness, and meditation to increase self-reflection.
Feedback: Utilizing feedback from others to gain insights into personal behaviors and emotions.
Self-Regulation Strategies:

Emotional Regulation Techniques: Teaching deep breathing, progressive muscle relaxation, and cognitive reframing.
Impulse Control: Helping clients develop strategies to manage impulsive behaviors and responses.
Motivation Enhancement:

Intrinsic Motivation: Identifying and fostering internal drivers such as personal values and passions.
Goal Alignment: Setting meaningful goals that align with the client's values and motivations.
Building Empathy:

Perspective-Taking Exercises: Encouraging clients to see situations from others' viewpoints.
Active Listening Skills: Teaching and practicing active listening to understand others' emotions and needs.
Improving Social Skills:

Communication Skills Training: Enhancing verbal and non-verbal communication skills.
Conflict Resolution: Teaching strategies for resolving conflicts constructively and maintaining healthy relationships.
Cultivating Self-Awareness
Role of Self-Awareness in Coaching:

Self-awareness is foundational to personal growth and emotional intelligence.
Coaches help clients explore and understand their thoughts, feelings, and behaviors.
Techniques for Increasing Self-Awareness:

Mindfulness Practices: Teaching mindfulness meditation and mindful living to heighten present-moment awareness.
Personality Assessments: Utilizing tools like the Myers-Briggs Type Indicator (MBTI) or the Big Five Personality Traits to gain insights.

Reflective Questioning: Using open-ended questions to encourage deep self-exploration and insight.
Cultural Sensitivity and Diversity in Mental Health Coaching
Understanding Cultural Sensitivity
Definition and Importance:

Cultural sensitivity involves being aware of and respecting cultural differences in beliefs, practices, and values.
It is crucial for providing effective and respectful mental health coaching to diverse populations.
Impact on Mental Health:

Cultural background influences how individuals perceive mental health, seek help, and respond to coaching.
Culturally sensitive coaching acknowledges and integrates these differences into the coaching process.
Strategies for Culturally Sensitive Coaching
Cultural Competence Development:

Education and Training: Engaging in ongoing education about different cultures and their impact on mental health.
Self-Reflection: Reflecting on one's own cultural biases and assumptions to provide unbiased coaching.
Building Trust and Rapport:

Respectful Communication: Using language and behaviors that show respect for clients' cultural backgrounds.
Cultural Matching: When possible, matching clients with coaches who share or understand their cultural background.
Tailoring Coaching Approaches:

Cultural Adaptation: Adapting coaching techniques to align with clients' cultural values and beliefs.
Inclusive Practices: Incorporating culturally relevant examples, metaphors, and practices in coaching sessions.
Case Examples Highlighting Cultural Competence

Example 1: Working with Immigrant Populations:

Understanding the unique stressors and mental health challenges faced by immigrants.
Tailoring coaching approaches to address issues such as acculturation stress, language barriers, and family dynamics.
Example 2: Supporting LGBTQ+ Clients:

Recognizing the specific mental health challenges related to identity, discrimination, and social support.
Creating a safe and affirming coaching environment that respects and celebrates diversity in sexual orientation and gender identity.
Example 3: Coaching in Multicultural Settings:

Adapting coaching practices to be effective in multicultural and multiethnic communities.
Using culturally relevant materials and resources to enhance the coaching experience.
Conclusion
Enhancing emotional intelligence and self-awareness is crucial for personal growth, mental health, and effective coaching. Additionally, integrating cultural sensitivity and diversity into mental health coaching ensures that coaching practices are inclusive, respectful, and effective across diverse populations. This chapter underscores the importance of these elements and provides practical strategies for coaches to implement in their work.

Chapter 31: Understanding Cultural Influences on Mental Health and Tailoring Coaching Approaches for Diverse Populations

Understanding Cultural Influences on Mental Health
Definition of Culture and Its Impact:

Culture encompasses the beliefs, values, customs, and behaviors shared by a group of people, which can significantly impact mental health.
It shapes how individuals perceive and experience mental health issues, seek help, and respond to treatment and coaching.
Cultural Variations in Mental Health Perceptions:

Different cultures have unique ways of understanding and expressing mental health concerns.
Some cultures may stigmatize mental health issues, leading to underreporting and reluctance to seek help.
Cultural beliefs can influence the types of symptoms individuals experience and how they interpret these symptoms.
Influence of Cultural Norms and Values:

Collectivist cultures may emphasize family and community support, while individualist cultures may prioritize personal autonomy and self-reliance.

Cultural norms around gender roles, spirituality, and coping mechanisms can affect mental health and well-being.

Examples of Cultural Influences:

In some Asian cultures, mental health issues may be viewed as a loss of face or shame, leading to a preference for somatic complaints over psychological ones.

Indigenous cultures might incorporate traditional healing practices and community rituals as part of mental health treatment.

Tailoring Coaching Approaches for Diverse Populations

Cultural Competence in Coaching:

Cultural competence involves understanding, respecting, and appropriately responding to the cultural contexts of clients. It is essential for creating an inclusive and effective coaching environment.

Strategies for Culturally Sensitive Coaching:

Cultural Awareness: Educating oneself about different cultures and their impact on mental health. This includes understanding cultural norms, values, and communication styles.

Active Listening: Paying close attention to clients' cultural backgrounds and experiences, and acknowledging their unique perspectives.

Respectful Inquiry: Asking clients about their cultural beliefs and practices in a respectful and non-judgmental manner.

Building Trust and Rapport with Diverse Clients:

Empathy and Understanding: Demonstrating empathy and understanding for clients' cultural experiences and challenges.

Inclusive Communication: Using language and communication styles that are respectful and inclusive of clients' cultural backgrounds.
Cultural Matching: When possible, matching clients with coaches who share or understand their cultural background to enhance rapport and trust.
Adapting Coaching Techniques:

Cultural Adaptation: Modifying coaching techniques and interventions to align with clients' cultural values and beliefs.
Flexible Approaches: Being open to incorporating clients' cultural practices and traditions into the coaching process.
Culturally Relevant Materials: Using examples, metaphors, and resources that are culturally relevant and resonate with clients' experiences.
Case Examples Highlighting Culturally Sensitive Coaching
Example 1: Working with Immigrant Populations:

Understanding the unique stressors and mental health challenges faced by immigrants, such as acculturation stress, language barriers, and family dynamics.
Tailoring coaching approaches to address these issues, such as providing language support and involving family members in the coaching process.
Example 2: Supporting LGBTQ+ Clients:

Recognizing the specific mental health challenges related to identity, discrimination, and social support.
Creating a safe and affirming coaching environment that respects and celebrates diversity in sexual orientation and gender identity.
Addressing internalized stigma and promoting self-acceptance and empowerment.
Example 3: Coaching in Multicultural Settings:

Adapting coaching practices to be effective in multicultural and multiethnic communities.
Using culturally relevant materials and resources to enhance the coaching experience.
Understanding the dynamics of multicultural interactions and promoting intercultural competence.
Conclusion
Understanding cultural influences on mental health and tailoring coaching approaches for diverse populations are crucial for effective mental health coaching. By incorporating cultural competence, coaches can provide more inclusive, respectful, and effective support to clients from various backgrounds. This chapter highlights the importance of cultural sensitivity and provides practical strategies for integrating it into mental health coaching practices.

Chapter 32: Case examples highlighting cultural competence in coaching.

Case Examples Highlighting Cultural Competence in Coaching
Example 1: Working with Immigrant Populations
Context:
A coach is working with a client who recently immigrated from a Southeast Asian country. The client is experiencing high levels of stress and anxiety related to acculturation, language barriers, and family separation.

Challenges:

The client feels isolated and struggles with cultural adjustments.
There is a significant language barrier that hinders effective communication.
The client is reluctant to discuss mental health issues due to cultural stigma.
Culturally Competent Approaches:

Language Support: The coach arranges for a professional interpreter to facilitate communication, ensuring the client feels understood and supported.

Cultural Sensitivity: The coach educates themselves about the client's cultural background and norms, showing respect for the client's values and beliefs.

Family Involvement: Understanding the importance of family in the client's culture, the coach encourages family participation in sessions when appropriate.

Stress Management Techniques: The coach introduces culturally appropriate stress management techniques, such as mindfulness practices that align with the client's spiritual beliefs.

Building Trust: The coach takes extra time to build rapport and trust, acknowledging the client's courage in seeking help and addressing the cultural stigma around mental health.

Outcome:

The client feels more comfortable and supported, leading to better engagement in the coaching process.

The client's stress levels decrease, and they develop effective coping strategies for acculturation challenges.

The involvement of family members enhances the client's support system and fosters a sense of community.

Example 2: Supporting LGBTQ+ Clients

Context:

A coach is working with a young adult client who identifies as non-binary and is struggling with identity issues, discrimination, and a lack of social support.

Challenges:

The client experiences discrimination and rejection from some family members and peers.

The client has internalized negative societal attitudes, leading to low self-esteem and self-acceptance issues.

The client is navigating the complexities of coming out in various social contexts.

Culturally Competent Approaches:

Affirming Environment: The coach creates a safe and affirming space for the client to express their identity without fear of judgment.

Identity Exploration: The coach supports the client in exploring and affirming their gender identity, using inclusive language and respecting their preferred pronouns.

Empathy and Understanding: The coach demonstrates empathy for the client's experiences of discrimination and validates their feelings.

Empowerment Strategies: The coach helps the client develop strategies for self-advocacy and resilience, encouraging them to connect with LGBTQ+ support groups and resources.

Family Dynamics: The coach works with the client to navigate family relationships, exploring ways to communicate their needs and set boundaries.

Outcome:

The client feels empowered and affirmed in their identity, leading to increased self-acceptance and confidence.

The client develops a strong support network through connections with LGBTQ+ communities.

The client gains effective communication skills for managing relationships with family and peers.

Example 3: Coaching in Multicultural Settings

Context:

A coach is working with a diverse group of clients from various ethnic backgrounds in a community mental health setting. The group includes individuals from African American, Latino, and Middle Eastern backgrounds.

Challenges:

Each client brings unique cultural perspectives, beliefs, and experiences to the group.
There may be differing views on mental health, stigma, and acceptable coping mechanisms.
Language barriers and different communication styles can complicate group dynamics.
Culturally Competent Approaches:

Cultural Education: The coach invests time in learning about the cultural backgrounds and mental health perspectives of each group member.
Inclusive Practices: The coach uses inclusive language and ensures that all group activities and discussions are culturally relevant and respectful.
Group Dynamics: The coach fosters an inclusive group environment where all members feel valued and heard, encouraging mutual respect and understanding.
Flexible Techniques: The coach adapts coaching techniques to align with the cultural preferences and values of the group members, integrating culturally specific coping strategies.
Community Engagement: The coach collaborates with community leaders and organizations to provide additional support and resources tailored to the cultural needs of the group.
Outcome:

The group members feel respected and understood, leading to enhanced engagement and participation.
The diverse perspectives enrich the group experience, fostering mutual learning and support.
The group members develop effective coping strategies that are culturally relevant and aligned with their values.
Conclusion

These case examples illustrate the importance of cultural competence in mental health coaching. By understanding and respecting the cultural contexts of clients, coaches can provide more effective and inclusive support, leading to better outcomes and enhanced well-being for diverse populations.

Chapter 33: Integrating Technology and Innovation in Mental Health Coaching

Integrating Technology and Innovation in Mental Health Coaching
The Role of Technology in Mental Health Coaching
Introduction to Digital Platforms:

Digital platforms have revolutionized the accessibility and delivery of mental health coaching services.
They offer clients flexible and convenient ways to engage with coaches, breaking down geographical and time barriers.
Types of Digital Platforms:

Telehealth Services: Video conferencing tools like Zoom and Skype enable face-to-face sessions remotely.
Mobile Apps: Coaching apps provide tools for setting goals, tracking progress, and communicating with coaches.

Online Courses and Webinars: These platforms offer structured coaching programs and educational resources.
Social Media Groups: Online communities on platforms like Facebook and LinkedIn provide peer support and resource sharing.
Advantages of Technology in Mental Health Coaching
Increased Accessibility:

Clients in remote or underserved areas can access high-quality coaching services.
Clients with busy schedules can find time for coaching sessions that fit their lifestyles.
Enhanced Engagement:

Interactive tools and resources, such as videos, quizzes, and digital worksheets, keep clients engaged.
Regular digital communication through messaging apps or platforms maintains client-coach connection between sessions.
Data-Driven Insights:

Digital platforms can track clients' progress, mood, and behaviors through automated data collection.
Coaches can use this data to tailor their approaches and measure the effectiveness of interventions.
Cost-Effectiveness:

Reduced overhead costs for both clients and coaches, making services more affordable.
Group coaching sessions and online courses can be more economical than traditional one-on-one sessions.
AI and Machine Learning in Mental Health Coaching
Personalized Coaching:

AI algorithms analyze clients' data to provide personalized coaching plans and recommendations.

Machine learning models can predict clients' needs and suggest tailored interventions.
Virtual Coaches:

AI-powered virtual coaches provide 24/7 support, offering immediate assistance and guidance.
These virtual assistants can handle routine queries, allowing human coaches to focus on more complex issues.
Chatbots and Conversational AI:

Chatbots facilitate continuous engagement, offering motivational messages, reminders, and check-ins.
They can guide clients through exercises and interventions, enhancing the coaching process.
Ethical Considerations and Data Privacy
Confidentiality and Privacy:

Ensuring the confidentiality of client data is paramount in digital coaching.
Coaches must use secure, HIPAA-compliant platforms to protect client information.
Informed Consent:

Clients should be informed about how their data will be used, stored, and protected.
Coaches must obtain explicit consent before collecting or using client data.
Algorithmic Bias:

Awareness of potential biases in AI algorithms that could affect coaching recommendations.
Continuous monitoring and updating of algorithms to ensure fairness and accuracy.
Balancing Innovation and Human Touch:

While technology enhances coaching, maintaining the human touch is crucial for building trust and rapport.
Coaches should blend digital tools with empathetic, personalized interactions.
Case Examples of Technology-Enhanced Coaching
Example 1: Telehealth Coaching for Rural Clients:

A coach uses video conferencing to work with clients in rural areas, providing access to mental health coaching that would otherwise be unavailable.
Clients appreciate the convenience and accessibility, leading to improved mental health outcomes.
Example 2: Mobile App for Anxiety Management:

A coach collaborates with a developer to create a mobile app that includes breathing exercises, mindfulness practices, and journaling prompts for clients with anxiety.
Clients use the app daily, reporting decreased anxiety levels and increased mindfulness.
Example 3: AI-Powered Progress Tracking:

A coach uses an AI-powered platform that tracks clients' moods and activities, providing real-time feedback and personalized recommendations.
Clients benefit from data-driven insights and customized coaching plans that evolve with their needs.
The Future of Technology in Mental Health Coaching
Emerging Trends:

The integration of virtual reality (VR) and augmented reality (AR) for immersive coaching experiences.
The use of biometric data (e.g., heart rate, sleep patterns) to inform coaching interventions.
Potential Challenges:

Addressing digital divide issues to ensure equitable access to technology-enhanced coaching.
Navigating the balance between technological innovation and maintaining the core human elements of coaching.
Conclusion:

Technology and innovation are transforming mental health coaching, offering new opportunities for accessibility, engagement, and personalization.
By integrating digital tools with ethical and culturally sensitive practices, coaches can enhance their impact and reach more clients effectively.

Chapter 34: Telehealth and digital platforms in coaching

Telehealth and Digital Platforms in Coaching
Introduction to Telehealth and Digital Platforms
What is Telehealth?

Telehealth refers to the use of digital communication technologies, such as video conferencing, messaging apps, and online platforms, to deliver health-related services and information.
In the context of mental health coaching, telehealth enables coaches to conduct sessions remotely, making services more accessible and convenient for clients.
The Rise of Digital Platforms:

Digital platforms for mental health coaching include specialized apps, websites, and software designed to facilitate coaching interactions, track progress, and provide resources. These platforms range from comprehensive telehealth systems to niche apps focusing on specific aspects of mental health and well-being.

Benefits of Telehealth and Digital Platforms

Accessibility:

Telehealth breaks down geographical barriers, allowing clients in remote or underserved areas to access mental health coaching.

It provides flexibility in scheduling, accommodating clients with busy or irregular schedules.

Convenience:

Clients can engage in coaching sessions from the comfort of their own homes, reducing the need for travel and making it easier to fit sessions into their daily routines.

Digital platforms often offer asynchronous communication options, such as messaging or email, for continuous support between sessions.

Cost-Effectiveness:

Telehealth reduces overhead costs for coaches, potentially lowering fees for clients.

Group coaching and online courses available on digital platforms can be more affordable alternatives to traditional one-on-one sessions.

Enhanced Engagement and Monitoring:

Digital tools such as apps and online portals can provide clients with interactive resources, reminders, and progress tracking features.

Coaches can monitor clients' progress in real-time and adjust coaching strategies based on data collected through digital platforms.

Key Features of Effective Digital Platforms

Secure Communication:

Platforms should offer encrypted and secure communication channels to ensure client confidentiality and privacy. Compliance with regulations like HIPAA (Health Insurance Portability and Accountability Act) is essential for protecting sensitive client information.

User-Friendly Interface:

Digital platforms should be intuitive and easy to navigate for both coaches and clients, minimizing technical barriers. Accessible design features, such as large text and clear instructions, can enhance user experience.

Integrated Tools and Resources:

Effective platforms provide a range of tools, including goal-setting modules, mood trackers, and journaling features. Access to educational resources, such as articles, videos, and webinars, can support clients' learning and development.

Real-Time Analytics and Feedback:

Platforms with real-time analytics allow coaches to track clients' progress, identify patterns, and make data-driven decisions. Automated feedback and reminders can keep clients engaged and motivated.

Examples of Digital Platforms in Mental Health Coaching

Telehealth Systems:

Platforms like BetterHelp and Talkspace offer comprehensive telehealth services, connecting clients with licensed coaches and therapists via video, phone, and messaging.

These systems often include assessment tools, progress tracking, and secure communication features.
Mobile Apps:

Apps like Headspace and Calm provide mindfulness and stress management resources, integrating guided meditations, breathing exercises, and sleep aids.
Coaching-specific apps like Coach.me offer goal-setting and habit-tracking tools, with options for virtual coaching support.
Online Courses and Webinars:

Platforms such as Udemy and Coursera offer online courses on mental health topics, including personal development and emotional intelligence.
Webinars hosted on platforms like Zoom or GoToWebinar allow coaches to reach larger audiences with interactive sessions on various mental health topics.
Social Media and Community Platforms:

Facebook groups, Reddit forums, and LinkedIn communities provide spaces for peer support, resource sharing, and networking among coaches and clients.
These platforms can facilitate group coaching sessions and foster a sense of community and belonging.
Ethical Considerations in Telehealth Coaching
Privacy and Confidentiality:

Coaches must ensure that the digital platforms they use comply with privacy regulations and provide secure communication channels.
Clients should be informed about how their data will be collected, stored, and used.
Informed Consent:

Obtaining informed consent is crucial when using telehealth and digital platforms, ensuring clients understand the risks and benefits.
Clear communication about the limits of confidentiality and the use of digital tools is essential.
Maintaining Professional Boundaries:

Coaches should establish and maintain professional boundaries, even when using digital communication tools.
Setting expectations for response times and communication methods can help maintain professional relationships.
Future Directions in Telehealth and Digital Platforms
Integration of AI and Machine Learning:

Advanced AI algorithms can provide personalized coaching recommendations, track progress, and predict clients' needs.
Machine learning models can enhance the accuracy and effectiveness of coaching interventions.
Virtual and Augmented Reality:

Emerging technologies like virtual reality (VR) and augmented reality (AR) offer immersive coaching experiences, such as virtual environments for relaxation or exposure therapy.
These technologies can enhance engagement and provide innovative ways to address mental health challenges.
Expanded Access and Inclusivity:

Efforts to bridge the digital divide and ensure equitable access to telehealth services are essential for reaching diverse populations.
Inclusive design and culturally sensitive approaches can enhance the effectiveness of digital platforms for all clients.
Conclusion:

Telehealth and digital platforms are transforming the landscape of mental health coaching, offering new opportunities for accessibility, engagement, and personalization.
By integrating ethical practices, innovative technologies, and user-friendly features, coaches can enhance their impact and support clients more effectively in their mental health journeys.

Chapter 35: AI and machine learning applications in mental health coaching

AI and Machine Learning Applications in Mental Health Coaching
Introduction to AI and Machine Learning in Mental Health Coaching
Understanding AI and Machine Learning:

Artificial Intelligence (AI) refers to the simulation of human intelligence processes by machines, particularly computer systems.

Machine Learning (ML) is a subset of AI, involving the use of algorithms and statistical models that enable computers to improve their performance on a task with data over time without being explicitly programmed.

Relevance to Mental Health Coaching:

AI and ML can analyze vast amounts of data to identify patterns, make predictions, and offer personalized recommendations, enhancing the effectiveness and efficiency of mental health coaching.

These technologies can support coaches in providing tailored interventions, tracking progress, and improving client outcomes.

Key Applications of AI and Machine Learning in Mental Health Coaching

Personalized Coaching Recommendations:

AI algorithms can analyze client data, including mood logs, behavioral patterns, and feedback from coaching sessions, to offer personalized coaching strategies.

These recommendations can help coaches tailor their approach to each client's unique needs, preferences, and goals.

Predictive Analytics:

Machine learning models can predict potential mental health issues or challenges based on historical data and behavioral trends.

Predictive analytics can enable early intervention, helping coaches address issues before they escalate.

Automated Progress Tracking:

AI-driven tools can automatically track and analyze clients' progress over time, providing insights into their improvement and areas needing attention.
Automated tracking can free up coaches to focus on client interaction and strategy rather than administrative tasks.
Virtual Coaching Assistants:

AI-powered virtual assistants can provide support between sessions, offering reminders, motivational messages, and resources.
These assistants can maintain client engagement and adherence to coaching plans, enhancing overall outcomes.
Natural Language Processing (NLP):

NLP, a branch of AI, enables computers to understand and respond to human language. In mental health coaching, NLP can analyze text from client communications to detect emotional cues and sentiment.
NLP tools can help coaches understand clients' underlying emotions and tailor their responses accordingly.
AI-Enhanced Self-Help Tools:

AI applications, such as chatbots and virtual reality experiences, offer self-help tools that clients can use independently.
These tools can provide coping strategies, relaxation exercises, and educational content, complementing the coaching process.
Examples of AI and Machine Learning Tools in Mental Health Coaching
Woebot:

Woebot is an AI-powered chatbot that uses cognitive-behavioral therapy (CBT) techniques to help users manage mental health issues such as anxiety and depression.

It engages in text-based conversations with users, offering support and practical advice.
Ginger:

Ginger provides on-demand mental health coaching through its app, utilizing AI to match clients with appropriate coaches and resources.
The platform uses ML to analyze user data and personalize the coaching experience.
Youper:

Youper employs AI and NLP to provide emotional health assistance, guiding users through conversations to help them understand and manage their emotions.
The app offers insights based on user interactions and tracks progress over time.
Benefits of AI and Machine Learning in Mental Health Coaching
Scalability and Accessibility:

AI and ML technologies can scale coaching services to reach a larger audience, including those in remote or underserved areas.
Digital tools can offer 24/7 support, making mental health resources accessible anytime and anywhere.
Efficiency and Consistency:

Automated processes reduce the administrative burden on coaches, allowing them to focus more on client interaction.
AI tools provide consistent support, ensuring that clients receive reliable guidance and resources.
Data-Driven Insights:

AI and ML can analyze large datasets to uncover trends and insights that might be missed by human coaches.

These insights can inform more effective coaching strategies and interventions.
Personalization:

AI's ability to analyze individual data points allows for highly personalized coaching plans.
Clients receive interventions tailored to their specific needs, enhancing the likelihood of positive outcomes.
Ethical Considerations and Challenges
Privacy and Data Security:

Ensuring the confidentiality and security of client data is paramount. Coaches and platform developers must comply with data protection regulations.
Transparent communication about data use and storage practices is essential to maintain client trust.
Bias and Fairness:

AI algorithms can inadvertently perpetuate biases present in training data, leading to unequal treatment of clients.
Ongoing evaluation and adjustment of AI models are necessary to ensure fairness and inclusivity.
Human Touch and Empathy:

While AI can enhance mental health coaching, the human element remains irreplaceable. Empathy, understanding, and nuanced judgment are critical components of effective coaching.
Balancing the use of AI with human interaction ensures that clients receive compassionate and holistic care.
Informed Consent:

Clients should be informed about the use of AI in their coaching process and give explicit consent.

Clear explanations of how AI tools work and their potential benefits and limitations are necessary for informed decision-making.
Future Directions in AI and Machine Learning for Mental Health Coaching
Advancements in AI Technology:

Continued improvements in AI and ML algorithms will enhance the accuracy and effectiveness of coaching tools. Innovations in deep learning and neural networks may offer more sophisticated and nuanced support.
Integration with Wearable Technology:

AI can integrate with wearable devices to monitor physiological data, such as heart rate and sleep patterns, providing real-time insights into clients' mental health.
This integration can enable more proactive and responsive coaching interventions.
Collaborative AI Systems:

AI systems that facilitate collaboration between multiple coaches and healthcare providers can offer a more comprehensive approach to client care.
Collaborative tools can ensure that clients receive coordinated and multidisciplinary support.
Personalized AI Coaches:

The development of AI coaches that adapt to individual clients' communication styles and preferences can enhance engagement and effectiveness.
These AI coaches can offer a more personalized and relatable experience for clients.
Ethical AI Development:

Ongoing research and dialogue about ethical AI development will ensure that mental health coaching technologies are designed and implemented responsibly.

Emphasizing transparency, accountability, and client well-being will guide the ethical evolution of AI in mental health coaching.

Conclusion

AI and machine learning are revolutionizing the field of mental health coaching, offering new opportunities for personalized, scalable, and data-driven support. By integrating these technologies thoughtfully and ethically, mental health coaches can enhance their practice and better serve their clients, fostering greater well-being and resilience in an increasingly digital world.

Chapter 36: Ethical considerations and data privacy concerns

Ethical Considerations and Data Privacy Concerns
Importance of Ethics in Mental Health Coaching
Client Trust and Safety:

Establishing and maintaining client trust is paramount in mental health coaching. Ethical considerations ensure that clients feel safe and respected, which is essential for effective coaching.
Professional Integrity:

Adhering to ethical guidelines upholds the integrity of the coaching profession. Coaches must demonstrate honesty, transparency, and accountability in their practice.
Legal Compliance:

Compliance with legal standards and regulations is crucial to protect both clients and coaches from legal repercussions. Ethical practices help ensure adherence to laws governing mental health services.
Key Ethical Considerations for Mental Health Coaches
Confidentiality:

Coaches must protect client confidentiality, ensuring that personal information and session details are kept private unless the client provides explicit consent to share specific information.

Confidentiality agreements and secure communication channels are essential components of maintaining privacy.
Informed Consent:

Clients should be fully informed about the coaching process, including the methods used, potential risks and benefits, and their rights. Obtaining informed consent ensures that clients willingly and knowingly participate in coaching.
Competence and Professional Development:

Coaches must be adequately trained and certified in mental health coaching techniques. Ongoing professional development is necessary to stay updated with the latest practices and ethical standards.
Coaches should only practice within their areas of competence and refer clients to other professionals when issues fall outside their expertise.
Dual Relationships and Boundaries:

Maintaining clear boundaries between the coach-client relationship and other personal or professional relationships is crucial. Dual relationships can lead to conflicts of interest and compromise the objectivity and effectiveness of coaching.
Non-Discrimination and Cultural Sensitivity:

Coaches must respect and accommodate clients' diverse backgrounds, including culture, race, gender, sexual orientation, and socioeconomic status.
Tailoring coaching approaches to be culturally sensitive ensures inclusivity and effectiveness.
Transparency and Honesty:

Coaches should be transparent about their qualifications, fees, and the scope of their services. Misrepresentation can damage client trust and the coaching profession's reputation.

Honest communication about the potential outcomes and limitations of coaching is essential.
Avoiding Harm:

The primary goal of mental health coaching is to benefit the client. Coaches must avoid actions or advice that could cause harm or exacerbate mental health issues.
Ethical decision-making frameworks can help coaches navigate complex situations to minimize the risk of harm.
Data Privacy Concerns in Mental Health Coaching
Data Collection and Storage:

Collecting only necessary data and storing it securely is vital to protect client privacy. Coaches should use encrypted and secure systems for storing client records and session notes.
Access to client data should be restricted to authorized personnel only, with robust authentication mechanisms in place.
Digital Communication and Telehealth:

With the rise of telehealth and digital platforms, ensuring secure communication channels is crucial. Using encrypted video conferencing tools and secure messaging platforms can protect client information.
Coaches should inform clients about the potential risks of digital communication and obtain their consent to use these methods.
Data Sharing and Third Parties:

Sharing client data with third parties, such as other healthcare providers or insurance companies, requires explicit client consent. Coaches should inform clients about who will have access to their data and for what purposes.
Data-sharing agreements should outline the responsibilities and protections in place to safeguard client information.
Anonymity and De-Identification:

When using client data for research, case studies, or training purposes, coaches must anonymize or de-identify the information to protect client identity.
Ensuring that client data cannot be traced back to individuals is essential for ethical practice.
Compliance with Data Protection Regulations:

Coaches must comply with data protection regulations, such as the General Data Protection Regulation (GDPR) in Europe or the Health Insurance Portability and Accountability Act (HIPAA) in the United States.
Understanding and adhering to these regulations help protect client data and avoid legal penalties.
Responding to Data Breaches:

Having a clear plan for responding to data breaches is critical. Coaches should notify affected clients promptly and take steps to mitigate any potential harm.
Regular audits and security assessments can help prevent data breaches and ensure ongoing compliance with data privacy standards.
Conclusion
Ethical considerations and data privacy concerns are integral to the practice of mental health coaching. By adhering to ethical guidelines and prioritizing client confidentiality and data security, coaches can build trust, uphold professional standards, and provide effective, responsible coaching services. Embracing these principles ensures that mental health coaching remains a valuable and respected field, dedicated to enhancing clients' well-being and resilience.

Chapter 37: Coaching Ethics and Professional Standards

Coaching Ethics and Professional Standards
Ethical guidelines form the cornerstone of effective mental health coaching, ensuring professionalism, client trust, and successful outcomes. Here are key considerations:

1. Client Confidentiality:

Confidentiality Agreement: Coaches must prioritize client privacy, maintaining confidentiality unless legally required to disclose information.
Secure Communication: Utilizing encrypted platforms for client communication ensures data security and trust.
2. Informed Consent:

Transparent Communication: Coaches clarify coaching objectives, methods, and potential outcomes upfront.
Client Autonomy: Clients have the right to understand and consent to coaching processes, fostering a collaborative and empowering coaching relationship.
3. Competence and Professionalism:

Continuous Learning: Coaches commit to ongoing professional development to enhance skills and stay updated on best practices.

Scope of Practice: Coaches work within their competencies, referring clients to specialists when needed, ensuring client welfare.
4. Boundary Management:

Clear Boundaries: Coaches maintain professional boundaries to avoid conflicts of interest and protect client interests.
Dual Relationships: Coaches refrain from dual relationships that could impair objectivity or exploit the coaching relationship.
5. Cultural Sensitivity:

Respect for Diversity: Coaches acknowledge and respect cultural, religious, and individual differences, adapting coaching approaches accordingly.
Inclusive Practices: Cultural competence enhances coaching effectiveness and fosters trust and understanding.
6. Accountability and Integrity:

Ethical Decision-Making: Coaches use ethical frameworks to navigate complex situations, prioritizing client welfare and ethical standards.
Professional Accountability: Coaches uphold ethical standards, promoting trust and credibility within the coaching profession.
7. Legal Compliance:

Regulatory Adherence: Coaches comply with relevant laws and regulations governing mental health services, safeguarding client rights and protections.
Data Protection: Coaches ensure secure handling of client data, respecting privacy and confidentiality obligations.
Conclusion:

Ethical coaching practices are foundational to client-centered care, promoting trust, professionalism, and positive outcomes. By adhering to ethical guidelines and maintaining high standards of practice, coaches uphold the integrity of the coaching profession and support clients in achieving meaningful personal growth and well-being.

Chapter 38: Ethical Guidelines for Mental Health Coaches

Maintaining Boundaries and Confidentiality
1. Client Confidentiality:

Confidentiality Agreement: Mental health coaches uphold strict confidentiality agreements, ensuring that all client information shared during sessions remains private and secure.
Limits of Confidentiality: Coaches clarify the limits of confidentiality upfront, explaining situations where disclosure may be required by law (e.g., imminent danger to self or others).
2. Boundaries in the Coaching Relationship:

Professional Boundaries: Coaches establish and maintain clear boundaries in their relationships with clients to prevent conflicts of interest or dual relationships.
Objectivity: Maintaining professional distance allows coaches to provide objective guidance and support without personal bias.
3. Informed Consent:

Clear Communication: Coaches obtain informed consent from clients, explaining the coaching process, goals, and methods comprehensively.
Client Autonomy: Clients have the right to understand and consent to coaching practices, ensuring they actively participate in decisions affecting their mental health.
Legal Considerations and Responsibilities
Regulatory Compliance
1. Legal Standards:

Adherence to Laws: Mental health coaches adhere to local, state, and federal laws governing the practice of mental health services, including data protection laws (e.g., HIPAA in the United States).
Professional Licensing: Coaches maintain necessary licenses and certifications required to practice legally within their jurisdiction.
2. Duty of Care:

Client Welfare: Coaches prioritize client welfare, ensuring their practices align with ethical standards and legal obligations.
Risk Management: Coaches identify and mitigate risks associated with coaching practices, protecting clients from harm and ensuring a safe coaching environment.
3. Documentation and Record-Keeping:

Accuracy and Security: Coaches maintain accurate and secure records of client interactions and progress, complying with legal requirements for data storage and confidentiality.
Client Access: Clients have the right to access their records and request corrections as per legal regulations.
Conclusion:

Ethical guidelines and legal responsibilities are fundamental to maintaining professionalism and trust in mental health coaching. By upholding confidentiality, respecting boundaries, and complying with legal standards, coaches safeguard client welfare and uphold the integrity of the coaching profession.

Chapter 39: The Future of Mental Health Coaching

The future of mental health coaching is evolving rapidly, driven by advancements in technology, shifting societal attitudes towards mental health, and growing recognition of the benefits of preventive mental health care. Here are some key trends and innovations shaping the future of mental health coaching:

Emerging Trends
Integration of Technology:

Telehealth and Digital Platforms: Increasing use of telehealth platforms and digital tools allows coaches to reach clients remotely, enhancing accessibility and convenience.
AI and Machine Learning: Utilization of AI-driven tools for personalized coaching experiences, predictive analytics for mental health assessments, and chatbots for ongoing support and monitoring.

Personalized and Holistic Approaches:

Precision Coaching: Tailoring coaching interventions based on individual needs, preferences, and personality traits using data-driven insights.
Holistic Wellness: Integrating physical health, nutrition, sleep, and mindfulness practices into coaching programs to promote overall well-being.
Evidence-Based Practices:

Emphasis on Outcomes: Increasing focus on measurable outcomes and evidence-based interventions to demonstrate coaching effectiveness and ensure client satisfaction.
Collaboration with Healthcare Providers: Closer collaboration with healthcare professionals, including psychologists, psychiatrists, and primary care providers, to provide integrated care.
Diversity and Cultural Competence:

Inclusive Coaching Practices: Addressing cultural and diversity considerations in coaching approaches to better serve diverse populations and reduce mental health disparities.
Cultural Sensitivity Training: Continued emphasis on training in cultural competence and sensitivity to enhance coaching effectiveness and client engagement.
Professionalization and Regulation:

Standardization of Training: Establishing clear standards and certifications for mental health coaches to ensure competency and professionalism.
Ethical Guidelines: Strengthening ethical guidelines and regulatory frameworks to protect client rights, ensure confidentiality, and maintain quality standards.
Community and Peer Support:

Group Coaching: Increasing popularity of group coaching formats for peer support, sharing experiences, and building resilience in a supportive community.

Online Support Networks: Expansion of online communities and forums where clients can connect, share resources, and receive ongoing support beyond coaching sessions.

Predictions for the Future

Technological Integration: Continued advancements in virtual reality (VR) and augmented reality (AR) for immersive therapeutic experiences and exposure therapy.

Preventive Mental Health: Shift towards preventive mental health strategies, focusing on early intervention, resilience-building, and stress management.

Global Accessibility: Expansion of mental health coaching services to underserved populations and remote areas through mobile apps, online platforms, and digital solutions.

Research and Innovation: Ongoing research into new interventions, therapies, and coaching models to address emerging mental health challenges and societal needs.

Conclusion

The future of mental health coaching is dynamic and promising, marked by technological innovation, personalized approaches, and a growing emphasis on holistic well-being. By embracing these trends and innovations, mental health coaches can play a pivotal role in promoting mental health resilience, improving access to care, and enhancing the overall quality of life for their clients.

Chapter 40: Emerging trends and innovations in coaching

Emerging trends and innovations in coaching are transforming the field, integrating new technologies, enhancing accessibility, and refining coaching methodologies. Here are some key trends shaping the future of coaching:

Technological Integration
Telehealth and Virtual Coaching:

Remote Accessibility: Increasing use of telehealth platforms for virtual coaching sessions, providing flexibility and accessibility for clients worldwide.
Virtual Reality (VR) and Augmented Reality (AR): Integration of VR/AR for immersive coaching experiences, particularly useful for simulations, skills training, and exposure therapy.
Artificial Intelligence (AI) and Machine Learning:

Personalized Coaching: AI-driven tools analyze client data to personalize coaching programs, offering tailored interventions and insights based on behavioral patterns and preferences.

Chatbots: AI-powered chatbots provide real-time support, coaching reminders, and behavioral nudges, enhancing client engagement and adherence to coaching goals.

Holistic Approaches

Wellness and Performance Coaching:

Holistic Wellness: Integration of physical health, nutrition, sleep, and mindfulness practices into coaching programs to optimize overall well-being.

Performance Coaching: Coaching aimed at enhancing performance in professional and personal domains, focusing on goal-setting, productivity, and skill development.

Evidence-Based Practices

Outcome Measurement and Data Analytics:

Metrics-Driven Coaching: Utilization of data analytics to track client progress, measure outcomes, and adjust coaching strategies based on evidence of effectiveness.

Research Integration: Incorporation of evidence-based practices and interventions supported by research findings to enhance coaching efficacy and client satisfaction.

Cultural Competence and Diversity

Cultural Sensitivity in Coaching:

Diverse Populations: Training coaches in cultural competence to effectively serve diverse populations, adapting coaching approaches to respect cultural norms and values.

Inclusivity: Promoting inclusivity in coaching practices, addressing societal disparities and promoting social equity through coaching interventions.

Professional Development and Standards

Continued Education and Certification:

Professionalization: Establishment of standards and certifications to ensure coaching competency, ethics, and adherence to professional guidelines.

Advanced Training: Specialized coaching certifications and ongoing education in niche areas such as health coaching, executive coaching, and leadership development.

Collaborative and Integrated Care

Collaboration with Healthcare Providers:

Integrated Care Models: Collaboration between coaches, therapists, and healthcare providers to offer integrated care plans, enhancing client support and treatment outcomes.

Referral Networks: Building networks with medical professionals to refer clients for specialized mental health or medical care as needed.

Conclusion

These emerging trends and innovations underscore the dynamic evolution of coaching as a profession. By embracing technology, enhancing cultural competence, and integrating evidence-based practices, coaches can effectively meet the diverse needs of clients and contribute to their overall well-being and personal growth. As coaching continues to evolve, staying informed about these trends and adapting practices accordingly will be crucial for maintaining relevance and effectiveness in the field.

Chapter 41: Predictions for the future of mental health coaching

Predicting the future of mental health coaching involves envisioning how the profession will evolve in response to technological advancements, societal shifts, and increasing demand for mental health support. Here are several predictions that could shape the future of mental health coaching:

Technological Integration:

Expansion of Telehealth: Telehealth platforms will become more sophisticated, offering seamless virtual coaching experiences with enhanced features like real-time analytics and secure communication channels.
AI and Virtual Reality: Artificial intelligence (AI) will play a larger role in personalized coaching, providing data-driven insights and virtual reality (VR) for immersive therapeutic environments and simulations.

Personalization and Precision Coaching:

Data-Driven Insights: Coaches will use advanced analytics to personalize coaching sessions based on individual client data, preferences, and behavioral patterns.
Precision Medicine Approach: Similar to healthcare, coaching will adopt a precision medicine approach, tailoring interventions to specific mental health needs and genetic predispositions.
Integration with Healthcare Systems:

Collaborative Care Models: Mental health coaches will work closely with healthcare providers, including psychiatrists and primary care physicians, to offer integrated care plans that address both physical and mental health needs.
Referral Networks: Coaches will build strong referral networks with medical professionals to ensure clients receive comprehensive care when necessary.
Focus on Prevention and Wellness:

Early Intervention. There will be a shift towards preventive mental health coaching, focusing on early detection of mental health issues and proactive interventions to promote resilience and well-being.
Wellness Coaching: Coaching programs will increasingly emphasize holistic wellness, incorporating nutrition, exercise, mindfulness, and stress management to optimize mental health outcomes.
Ethical and Regulatory Standards:

Standardization: There will be efforts to standardize training, certification, and ethical guidelines for mental health coaches to ensure professionalism, quality of care, and client safety.

Legal Considerations: Coaches will navigate evolving legal landscapes, including data privacy laws and telehealth regulations, to protect client confidentiality and uphold ethical standards.
Cultural Competence and Inclusivity:

Diversity Training: Coaches will receive specialized training in cultural competence to better serve diverse populations and address disparities in mental health care access and outcomes.
Inclusive Practices: Coaching approaches will become more inclusive and sensitive to varying cultural norms, values, and beliefs, fostering a more supportive and effective coaching relationship.
Research and Evidence-Based Practices:

Continuous Innovation: Coaching will continue to evolve based on emerging research findings and evidence-based practices, ensuring that interventions are grounded in scientific rigor and proven effectiveness.
Outcome Measurement: There will be increased emphasis on measuring coaching outcomes and client progress using standardized metrics and assessment tools to demonstrate efficacy and value.
In summary, the future of mental health coaching promises to be dynamic and transformative, driven by advancements in technology, a deeper understanding of mental health dynamics, and a commitment to personalized, holistic care. Coaches who adapt to these changes and embrace innovation will be well-positioned to meet the evolving needs of clients and contribute positively to mental health outcomes globally.

Chapter 42: Personal reflections and concluding thoughts.

In the realm of mental health coaching, personal reflections and concluding thoughts serve as a crucial moment to synthesize key insights and inspire further action. Here are some personal reflections and concluding thoughts that could encapsulate the essence of the journey through mental health coaching:

Throughout this exploration of mental health coaching, the profound impact of personalized support and evidence-based strategies has emerged as a beacon of hope in the realm of mental wellness. As I conclude this journey, several reflections come to mind:

Firstly, the power of human connection and empathy cannot be overstated. Witnessing clients navigate their challenges with resilience and grace reaffirms the transformative potential of coaching. Each individual's journey is unique, yet the universal desire for growth and well-being unites us all.

Secondly, the integration of cutting-edge technology has expanded our toolkit exponentially. From AI-driven insights to virtual reality simulations, these innovations enhance our ability to tailor interventions and meet clients where they are on their path to healing.

Ethical considerations remain paramount. Upholding confidentiality, maintaining boundaries, and navigating complex legal landscapes are foundational to ethical practice. As the field evolves, so too must our commitment to these principles.

Looking ahead, I envision a future where mental health coaching continues to evolve and thrive. By embracing diversity, fostering inclusivity, and advancing our understanding of the human psyche, we can forge a path towards a more compassionate and resilient society.

In closing, I invite you to carry forward the insights gleaned from these pages. Whether you are a coach, a client, or an advocate for mental health, your role in this collective journey is invaluable. Together, we can cultivate a future where mental well-being is prioritized, stigma is dismantled, and every individual has the opportunity to thrive.

Thank you for joining me on this transformative exploration. May it empower you to embark on your own path towards personal growth, resilience, and profound well-being.

Warm regards,

Laurel D. Malvern

Conclusion: Recap of key concepts and takeaways

In concluding our exploration of mental health coaching, several key concepts and takeaways emerge as pivotal to understanding and practicing this dynamic field:

Definition and Scope: Mental health coaching bridges the gap between therapy and counseling, focusing on personal growth, resilience, and well-being rather than clinical diagnosis and treatment.

Role and Responsibilities: A mental health coach acts as a supportive partner, guiding clients through challenges, fostering self-awareness, and empowering them to achieve their goals through structured sessions and evidence-based practices.

Foundations: Grounded in psychology and neuroscience, coaching integrates theories and insights into behavior change, emphasizing the impact of thoughts, emotions, and habits on mental health outcomes.

Techniques and Approaches: Cognitive Behavioral Coaching (CBC), positive psychology interventions, and mindfulness-based practices equip coaches with tools to address specific challenges like anxiety, depression, and addiction recovery.

Cultural Sensitivity: Tailoring coaching approaches to diverse cultural backgrounds ensures inclusivity and effectiveness, honoring individual beliefs and values in the coaching process.

Technological Integration: Embracing telehealth, AI-driven insights, and virtual platforms enhances accessibility and personalization, meeting clients' needs in an increasingly digital world.

Ethical Standards: Upholding confidentiality, maintaining professional boundaries, and navigating legal considerations are foundational to ethical coaching practice, ensuring client trust and safety.

Future Trends: Anticipating advancements in technology, research-driven practices, and collaborative care models positions mental health coaching at the forefront of holistic wellness and preventive mental health care.

In essence, mental health coaching empowers individuals to cultivate resilience, enhance emotional intelligence, and achieve personal growth. By integrating diverse perspectives, leveraging innovative tools, and upholding ethical standards, coaches play a vital role in promoting mental well-being and fostering a healthier, more connected society.

As we conclude, I encourage you to reflect on these insights and consider how mental health coaching can contribute to your journey towards fulfillment and thriving. Together, let us embrace the transformative potential of coaching to nurture resilience, cultivate well-being, and empower lives.

Warm regards,

Laurel D. Malvern

Call to Action: Embrace Your Journey with Mental Health Coaching

Are you ready to embark on a transformative journey towards personal growth, resilience, and well-being? Whether you're seeking to enhance your own mental health or explore a career in coaching, now is the time to take the next step. Here's how you can get started:

Explore Coaching Opportunities: Discover the diverse paths within mental health coaching, from supporting individuals through challenges to fostering wellness and resilience. Your unique skills and passions can make a profound difference in others' lives.

Educate Yourself: Dive deeper into the foundations of mental health coaching. Equip yourself with knowledge of psychology, neuroscience, and evidence-based practices that empower coaches to facilitate meaningful change.

Seek Guidance: Connect with experienced coaches and mentors who can offer insights and support as you navigate your journey. Their wisdom and guidance will enrich your understanding and skills in coaching practice.

Commit to Professional Development: Pursue certifications and ongoing education to ensure you uphold ethical standards and stay abreast of industry trends. Continuous learning enhances your effectiveness and credibility as a coach.

Embrace Technology: Embrace the potential of telehealth, AI-driven insights, and virtual platforms to expand your reach and impact. Harness these tools to personalize coaching experiences and meet the evolving needs of clients.

Advocate for Mental Health: Champion mental health awareness and destigmatization within your community and beyond. Your voice and advocacy can inspire others to prioritize their well-being and seek support when needed.

Take Action Today: Whether you're considering coaching as a career or exploring it for personal growth, take the first step towards your goals. Your journey with mental health coaching begins with a commitment to learning, growth, and making a positive difference in the lives of others.

Join us in shaping the future of mental health coaching—a future where resilience is nurtured, well-being is prioritized, and every individual has the support they need to thrive.

Appendix A: Resources for Further Reading

Books

Co-Active Coaching: Changing Business, Transforming Lives
by Henry Kimsey-House, Karen Kimsey-House, Phillip
Sandahl, and Laura Whitworth
The Art of Coaching: Effective Strategies for School
Transformation by Elena Aguilar
The Neuroscience of Change: A Compassion-Based Program
for Personal Transformation by Kelly McGonigal
Journals and Articles

International Journal of Evidence Based Coaching and
Mentoring
Journal of Positive Psychology
Websites

International Coach Federation (ICF) -
www.coachfederation.org
Positive Psychology Center - www.positivepsychology.com
Appendix B: Professional Development

Certification Programs

Certified Professional Coach (CPC) - International Coach
Federation (ICF)
Certified Wellness Coach (CWC) - Wellcoaches School of
Coaching
Workshops and Conferences

Annual Coaching Conference - International Coach Federation
(ICF)
Positive Psychology Summit - Positive Psychology Center
Online Courses

Coursera - Various courses on coaching and psychology
Udemy - Coaching certification courses and skill development

Appendix B: Glossary of Terms

Coaching

A collaborative process where a coach facilitates personal and professional growth in individuals by helping them to improve their performance and enhance the quality of their lives.
Mental Health Coaching

A specialized form of coaching focused on supporting individuals in improving their mental well-being, managing mental health challenges, and achieving personal goals related to mental wellness.
Cognitive Behavioral Coaching (CBC)

An approach that integrates cognitive behavioral techniques into coaching sessions to help individuals change unhelpful thoughts and behaviors that may contribute to mental health issues.
Positive Psychology

The scientific study of what makes life worth living, focusing on strengths, virtues, and factors that contribute to psychological well-being and resilience.
Mindfulness

The practice of being present in the moment, cultivating awareness of thoughts, feelings, and sensations without judgment, often used in coaching to promote stress reduction and emotional regulation.
Resilience

The ability to bounce back from adversity, adapt to change, and maintain well-being in the face of challenges.
Telehealth

The use of digital communication technologies, such as video conferencing and online platforms, to provide remote healthcare services, including mental health coaching sessions.

Ethical Guidelines

Standards of conduct and principles that guide professional behavior in coaching, emphasizing confidentiality, respect for client autonomy, and integrity.
AI and Machine Learning

Artificial Intelligence (AI) refers to machines performing tasks that typically require human intelligence, while Machine Learning (ML) enables AI systems to learn and improve from experience without being explicitly programmed.
Data Privacy

The protection of personal information collected, used, and stored by organizations, ensuring confidentiality and security in coaching interactions.

Appendix C: Sample Coaching Exercises and Worksheets

Goal-Setting Worksheet

Objective: Assist clients in clarifying their goals and creating actionable steps towards achieving them.
Instructions: Write down your long-term and short-term goals. Break them down into smaller, manageable steps. Set deadlines and identify potential obstacles. List resources and support needed to accomplish each goal.
Values Clarification Exercise

Objective: Help clients identify and prioritize their core values to align their actions and decisions with their authentic selves.
Instructions: Reflect on your values in various life domains (e.g., career, relationships, health). Rank them in order of importance. Consider how your current goals and actions align with these values. Are there any adjustments you need to make?
Mindfulness Practice

Objective: Introduce clients to mindfulness techniques to enhance self-awareness, reduce stress, and promote emotional regulation.
Instructions: Practice mindfulness by focusing on your breath for five minutes. Notice any thoughts or emotions that arise without judgment. Bring your attention back to your breath whenever your mind wanders.
Strengths Assessment

Objective: Help clients identify their strengths and leverage them to achieve personal and professional goals.
Instructions: Complete a strengths assessment tool (e.g., VIA Character Strengths Survey). Reflect on your top strengths. How can you use these strengths to overcome challenges and enhance your well-being?
Journaling Prompt: Gratitude Practice

Objective: Cultivate gratitude to promote positive emotions and resilience.

Instructions: Write down three things you are grateful for each day. Reflect on how these things contribute to your life and well-being. Notice any shifts in your mood or perspective over time.

Problem-Solving Worksheet

Objective: Guide clients through a structured process to identify problems, explore potential solutions, and make informed decisions.

Instructions: Define the problem you are facing. Brainstorm possible solutions. Evaluate each solution based on its feasibility and potential outcomes. Select the best solution and create an action plan to implement it.

Bonus Chapter 1: Integration of Advanced Technologies:

How has artificial intelligence and virtual reality transformed mental health coaching practices?

In the realm of mental health coaching, the integration of advanced technologies like artificial intelligence (AI) and virtual reality (VR) holds significant promise and potential impact:

Personalized Insights and Assessment: AI algorithms can analyze vast amounts of client data, including verbal cues, facial expressions, and physiological responses, to provide coaches with deeper insights into clients' emotional states and behavioral patterns. This data-driven approach enhances the accuracy of assessments and allows for more personalized coaching interventions.

Enhanced Accessibility: Virtual reality platforms can simulate therapeutic environments and scenarios, providing clients with immersive experiences to practice coping skills and confront fears in a controlled setting. This technology expands access to therapeutic interventions for individuals who may face geographical or logistical barriers to traditional coaching services.

Interactive Coaching Tools: AI-powered chatbots and virtual assistants can support ongoing coaching between sessions by providing reminders, goal tracking, and real-time feedback based on client input. These tools enhance accountability and engagement while extending the reach of coaching services beyond scheduled appointments.

Augmented Therapeutic Techniques: VR-based exposure therapies are increasingly used to treat phobias, PTSD, and anxiety disorders by immersing clients in virtual environments that provoke targeted emotional responses. Coaches can guide clients through these immersive experiences, fostering desensitization and emotional regulation skills in a controlled, safe environment.

Ethical Considerations and Data Privacy: As with any integration of technology in healthcare, ethical considerations regarding data privacy, informed consent, and algorithm biases must be carefully addressed. Coaches must uphold stringent ethical standards to protect client confidentiality and ensure that AI-driven insights are used responsibly and ethically in coaching practices.

Future Directions: Looking ahead, ongoing research and development in AI and VR are likely to refine these technologies further, potentially expanding their applications in mental health coaching. Collaborative efforts between technology developers, mental health professionals, and regulatory bodies will be crucial in maximizing the benefits of advanced technologies while safeguarding client well-being.

In summary, the integration of AI and VR technologies in mental health coaching represents a transformative shift towards more personalized, accessible, and effective interventions. While challenges and ethical considerations remain, these innovations hold the promise of enhancing therapeutic outcomes and expanding the reach of mental health support globally.

Bonus Chapter 2: Global Perspectives:

What are the cultural nuances and global best practices in mental health coaching, considering diverse populations and contexts?

In exploring global perspectives on mental health coaching, it becomes evident that cultural nuances and best practices vary significantly across diverse populations and contexts. Understanding these differences is essential for coaches aiming to provide effective support and interventions worldwide.

Cultural Sensitivity in Coaching: Cultural beliefs, values, and practices profoundly influence perceptions of mental health and help-seeking behaviors. Coaches must be attuned to these cultural nuances to build trust and rapport with clients from different backgrounds.

Tailoring Coaching Approaches: Best practices in coaching often involve adapting techniques to align with cultural norms and preferences. For example, collectivist cultures may prioritize community support and interdependence, while individualistic cultures may emphasize personal autonomy and achievement.

Language and Communication: Effective coaching requires clear communication, which may involve overcoming language barriers and utilizing culturally appropriate communication styles. Coaches should consider linguistic diversity and the impact of language on mental health discussions.

Stigma and Mental Health: Stigma surrounding mental health varies widely across cultures and can impact help-seeking behaviors. Coaches play a vital role in reducing stigma by fostering open dialogue and promoting mental health literacy within communities.

Integration of Traditional Practices: Many cultures integrate traditional healing practices, such as herbal remedies or spiritual rituals, alongside modern coaching approaches. Coaches may collaborate with traditional healers or incorporate culturally relevant strategies into their coaching plans.

Globalization and Urbanization: Urbanization and globalization trends influence mental health challenges and support needs worldwide. Coaches may encounter clients navigating rapid societal changes, economic pressures, and acculturation stress.

Ethical and Legal Considerations: Coaches operating internationally must navigate diverse legal frameworks and ethical standards governing mental health practice. Understanding local regulations and upholding ethical guidelines are crucial for maintaining professional integrity.

Collaborative Partnerships: Building partnerships with local stakeholders, including healthcare providers, community leaders, and policymakers, enhances the effectiveness and sustainability of mental health coaching initiatives globally.

Training and Education: Coaches benefit from ongoing training in cross-cultural competence and global mental health issues. Continuing education ensures coaches are equipped to navigate cultural complexities and deliver culturally competent care.

Future Directions: As mental health coaching continues to evolve globally, there is a growing need for research, collaboration, and innovation in addressing diverse populations' mental health needs. Coaches can contribute to advancing global mental health by advocating for inclusive practices and adapting to emerging trends.

This bonus chapter explores the rich diversity of cultural perspectives and practices in mental health coaching, emphasizing the importance of cultural competence, adaptation, and ethical awareness in providing effective support to clients worldwide.

Bonus Chapter 3: Environmental Influences:

How does climate change and environmental factors impact mental health, and what role can coach play in fostering resilience?

Climate change and environmental factors exert profound impacts on mental health, posing significant challenges and opportunities for mental health coaching to foster resilience in individuals and communities.

Psychological Impact of Climate Change: Rising temperatures, natural disasters, and environmental degradation contribute to heightened anxiety, stress, and trauma among populations globally. Coaching can help individuals cope with eco-anxiety, grief over environmental losses, and uncertainty about the future.

Vulnerable Populations: Marginalized communities, including those in low-income areas or regions disproportionately affected by environmental hazards, face heightened mental health risks. Coaches can support these populations by addressing systemic inequities, promoting community resilience, and advocating for environmental justice.

Adaptation and Coping Strategies: Coaching fosters adaptive coping strategies, such as mindfulness, stress management techniques, and goal-setting, to empower individuals in navigating environmental stressors. Clients learn to cultivate resilience by focusing on personal strengths and proactive responses to environmental challenges.

Community Resilience Building: Coaches facilitate community-based interventions that strengthen social cohesion, disaster preparedness, and collective coping mechanisms. By fostering supportive networks and shared resources, coaching enhances community resilience to environmental disruptions.

Educational and Advocacy Roles: Coaches play a crucial role in raising awareness about the mental health impacts of climate change, promoting eco-conscious behaviors, and advocating for policies that prioritize environmental sustainability and mental well-being.

Intersection with Health Equity: Environmental degradation exacerbates health disparities, impacting access to clean air, water, and safe living conditions. Coaches advocate for environmental health policies that address social determinants of mental health and promote health equity.

Personal and Planetary Well-being: Coaching encourages a holistic approach to well-being that integrates personal health goals with environmental stewardship. Clients explore ways to reduce their carbon footprint, support sustainable practices, and cultivate a sense of interconnectedness with the natural world.

Preventative and Therapeutic Support: Proactive coaching interventions provide preventative mental health support, reducing the risk of climate-related distress and promoting adaptive coping before crises occur. Therapeutic coaching models offer tailored support for individuals experiencing acute environmental stressors or trauma.

Research and Innovation: Ongoing research into the mental health impacts of climate change informs evidence-based coaching practices. Coaches contribute to innovative interventions that address emerging environmental challenges and promote adaptive resilience strategies.

Future Directions: As climate change continues to unfold, there is a growing imperative for coaches to integrate environmental considerations into mental health practice. Collaboration with environmental scientists, policymakers, and community stakeholders strengthens the role of coaching in fostering resilience amid environmental crises.

This bonus chapter explores the intersection of climate change, environmental factors, and mental health coaching, highlighting opportunities for resilience-building, advocacy, and transformative action in response to evolving environmental challenges.

Bonus Chapter 4: Digital Ethics in Mental Health Coaching

As digital platforms and data analytics play an increasingly integral role in mental health coaching, it becomes essential to navigate evolving ethical considerations to ensure client well-being and uphold professional standards.

Data Privacy and Confidentiality: Coaches must prioritize client confidentiality and secure data management practices when utilizing digital platforms for communication, assessment, and record-keeping. Adhering to international data protection regulations such as GDPR and HIPAA is critical to safeguarding client information.

Informed Consent and Transparency: Clients should be fully informed about how their data will be collected, used, and stored within digital coaching platforms. Coaches must obtain explicit consent and provide transparent disclosures regarding data analytics, AI algorithms, and third-party data sharing practices.

Algorithmic Bias and Fairness: AI-driven algorithms in coaching platforms may unintentionally perpetuate biases based on race, gender, or socioeconomic status, affecting assessment accuracy and treatment recommendations. Coaches should mitigate algorithmic bias through rigorous testing, diversity in dataset representation, and ongoing algorithm transparency.

Digital Literacy and Accessibility: Coaches promote digital literacy among clients to empower informed decision-making about using digital tools in coaching. Ensuring accessibility for individuals with disabilities is crucial, including adapting platforms for screen readers, alternative communication methods, and inclusive design practices.

Professional Boundaries in Virtual Settings: Establishing clear boundaries and guidelines for virtual coaching sessions is essential to maintain professionalism and client trust. Coaches navigate the challenges of building rapport, managing non-verbal cues, and ensuring session confidentiality in online environments.

Ethical Use of Behavioral Data: Analyzing behavioral data from digital platforms can provide valuable insights into client progress and needs. Coaches should use this data ethically, avoiding exploitation or manipulation, and empowering clients to interpret and act upon their own data insights.

Continuing Education and Ethical Guidelines: Coaches engage in ongoing education to stay abreast of evolving digital ethics guidelines and best practices. Professional organizations and regulatory bodies provide ethical frameworks and resources to guide ethical decision-making in digital mental health coaching.

Risk Assessment and Crisis Management: Digital platforms enable real-time monitoring of client well-being, including detecting signs of crisis or deterioration. Coaches implement protocols for crisis intervention, ensuring immediate support and referrals when necessary.

Collaboration with Tech Developers and Researchers: Coaches collaborate with technology developers, researchers, and ethicists to co-design responsible digital solutions that prioritize client safety, consent, and ethical use of data. Transparency and accountability are central to these partnerships.

Future Directions: As digital technologies continue to evolve, ethical considerations in mental health coaching will remain paramount. Coaches advocate for regulatory policies, industry standards, and interdisciplinary collaboration to advance ethical practices and protect client rights in the digital age.

This bonus chapter explores the complex landscape of digital ethics in mental health coaching, emphasizing the importance of ethical awareness, transparency, and client-centered care in leveraging digital platforms for transformative coaching interventions.

Bonus Chapter 5: Interdisciplinary Approaches in Mental Health Coaching

Incorporating insights from diverse disciplines such as neuroscience, behavioral economics, and sociology enhances the effectiveness and comprehensiveness of mental health coaching, fostering holistic client outcomes and addressing multifaceted challenges.

Neuroscience and Behavior Change: Neuroscience offers valuable insights into brain function, neuroplasticity, and behavioral change mechanisms. Coaches leverage neuroscientific principles to enhance interventions, such as promoting mindfulness for stress reduction or cognitive-behavioral strategies for habit formation.

Behavioral Economics in Decision-Making: Behavioral economics explores how cognitive biases, emotions, and social influences shape decision-making processes. Coaches apply behavioral economics principles to support clients in setting achievable goals, overcoming procrastination, and making sustainable behavior changes.

Sociological Perspectives on Well-being: Sociology examines the social determinants of health and well-being, including the impact of social networks, cultural norms, and socioeconomic factors. Coaches integrate sociological insights to address systemic barriers, foster social support networks, and promote community resilience.

Psychology and Counseling Integration: Coaches draw from psychological theories and counseling techniques to enhance client self-awareness, emotional regulation, and interpersonal skills. Integrating therapeutic modalities such as cognitive-behavioral therapy (CBT) or positive psychology interventions enriches coaching practice.

Systems Theory and Holistic Approaches: Systems theory considers individuals within the context of interconnected systems, including family dynamics, organizational culture, and community environments. Coaches adopt holistic approaches to understand clients' systemic influences and facilitate comprehensive well-being.

Biofeedback and Technology Applications: Biofeedback technologies provide real-time physiological data, empowering clients to self-regulate stress responses and improve emotional resilience. Coaches integrate biofeedback tools into coaching sessions to enhance awareness and self-management of mind-body interactions.

Cultural Competence and Diversity: Understanding cultural contexts and diverse identities enriches coaching practice, promoting culturally responsive interventions and inclusive care. Coaches adapt approaches to honor clients' cultural values, beliefs, and experiences, fostering trust and collaboration.

Interprofessional Collaboration: Coaches collaborate with professionals from diverse disciplines, including healthcare providers, educators, and community leaders. Interprofessional teams enhance holistic care coordination, address complex client needs, and promote integrated health and well-being solutions.

Research and Evidence-Based Practices: Coaches engage in interdisciplinary research to validate innovative approaches and evidence-based practices in mental health coaching. Integrating research findings enhances coaching efficacy, informs practice guidelines, and advances professional standards.

Future Directions and Innovation: Embracing interdisciplinary approaches propels mental health coaching into the future, driving innovation, and expanding the scope of client-centered care. Coaches advocate for interdisciplinary collaboration, lifelong learning, and continuous adaptation to optimize client outcomes.

This bonus chapter explores the synergistic integration of neuroscience, behavioral economics, sociology, and other interdisciplinary fields into mental health coaching. By embracing diverse perspectives and evidence-based practices, coaches enhance their ability to support clients holistically and promote sustainable well-being outcomes.

Bonus Chapter 6: Legal and Regulatory Landscape in Mental Health Coaching

Navigating the legal and regulatory frameworks is essential for mental health coaches to ensure ethical practice, client protection, and professional accountability across different jurisdictions worldwide.

Licensing and Certification Requirements: Understanding the licensure and certification requirements specific to mental health coaching in different countries and states is crucial. Coaches adhere to regulatory standards to legally practice and maintain professional competence.

Scope of Practice and Professional Boundaries: Clarifying the scope of practice delineates the roles, responsibilities, and limitations of mental health coaches compared to licensed therapists and counselors. Coaches uphold professional boundaries to safeguard client welfare and maintain ethical conduct.

Informed Consent and Confidentiality: Coaches obtain informed consent from clients, outlining the coaching process, goals, risks, and benefits. Confidentiality agreements protect client privacy, with exceptions outlined based on legal mandates, such as reporting harm or complying with court orders.

Data Protection and Privacy Laws: Adhering to data protection regulations, such as GDPR in Europe or HIPAA in the United States, ensures secure handling of client information, digital communications, and electronic records. Coaches implement robust data security measures and client confidentiality protocols.

Ethical Guidelines and Codes of Conduct: Professional organizations establish ethical guidelines and codes of conduct that govern mental health coaching practices. Coaches uphold ethical principles, including integrity, respect for autonomy, non-discrimination, and accountability to clients and stakeholders.

Risk Management and Crisis Intervention: Coaches develop risk management protocols to address emergencies, crises, or client harm indicators. Understanding legal obligations for reporting and intervening in critical situations ensures timely support and compliance with mandated reporting laws.

Telehealth and Digital Platforms: Integrating telehealth technologies requires adherence to regulatory standards governing remote service delivery, licensure reciprocity, and cross-border practice. Coaches navigate legal complexities to deliver virtual coaching services securely and ethically.

Professional Liability Insurance: Coaches obtain professional liability insurance to mitigate financial risks associated with allegations of malpractice, negligence, or misconduct. Insurance coverage supports legal defense costs and potential settlements arising from client disputes or claims.

Regulatory Updates and Compliance: Staying informed about evolving legal standards and regulatory updates is essential for maintaining compliance and adapting practice protocols accordingly. Coaches engage in continuing education and professional development to uphold current legal requirements.

Advocacy and Policy Engagement: Coaches advocate for legislative reforms, policy initiatives, and professional standards that promote client rights, practitioner well-being, and ethical practice in mental health coaching. Active engagement fosters a supportive regulatory environment and enhances public trust in coaching professions.

This bonus chapter provides an in-depth exploration of the legal and regulatory landscape shaping mental health coaching practices globally. Coaches navigate diverse legal frameworks, uphold ethical standards, and advocate for policies that prioritize client safety, professional integrity, and the advancement of coaching professions.

Bonus Chapter 7: Emerging Mental Health Challenges

The landscape of mental health is continually evolving, influenced by emerging societal issues that pose new challenges to individuals' well-being. Mental health coaches play a crucial role in addressing these complexities through tailored strategies and proactive interventions.

Social Media Addiction and Digital Wellness: As digital connectivity expands, social media addiction and digital overwhelm contribute to stress, anxiety, and social comparison. Coaches educate clients on mindful technology use, digital detox strategies, and cultivating healthy digital habits to promote mental balance.

Economic Uncertainty and Financial Stress: Economic fluctuations and financial insecurities impact mental health, exacerbating anxiety, depression, and relational strain. Coaches collaborate with clients to navigate financial challenges, develop resilience in career transitions, and foster adaptive coping strategies for financial wellness.

Environmental and Climate-Related Distress: Environmental changes, natural disasters, and eco-anxiety contribute to mental health concerns, including stress, grief, and existential uncertainty. Coaches facilitate resilience-building exercises, eco-awareness practices, and community engagement to support clients in processing environmental stressors.

Workplace Burnout and Career Transitions: High-pressure work environments, burnout, and job dissatisfaction affect mental well-being. Coaches empower clients with stress management techniques, career navigation skills, and work-life balance strategies to foster professional fulfillment and resilience in career transitions.

Loneliness and Social Isolation: Increasing rates of loneliness and social isolation impact mental health, contributing to depression, low self-esteem, and relational difficulties. Coaches facilitate social connection initiatives, interpersonal skills development, and community engagement to alleviate isolation and enhance emotional support networks.

Cultural and Identity-Based Stressors: Cultural discrimination, identity challenges, and acculturation stress influence mental health outcomes across diverse populations. Coaches integrate cultural competence, identity affirmation practices, and multicultural counseling approaches to support clients in navigating cultural stressors.

Health Disparities and Access to Care: Disparities in healthcare access and systemic inequities impact mental health outcomes, particularly among marginalized communities. Coaches advocate for health equity, collaborate with healthcare providers, and empower clients with advocacy skills to address barriers to mental health services.

Technological Advancements and Digital Health: Innovations in telehealth, artificial intelligence, and digital therapeutics revolutionize mental health care delivery. Coaches integrate digital health solutions, personalized apps, and virtual support networks to enhance accessibility, engagement, and outcomes in coaching practice.

Generational and Lifespan Challenges: From youth mental health concerns to aging-related transitions, coaches address lifespan challenges through age-appropriate coaching interventions, developmental guidance, and resilience-building strategies tailored to diverse generational needs.

Political Unrest and Societal Turbulence: Political polarization, social unrest, and global crises impact mental health by fostering uncertainty, fear, and community unrest. Coaches promote civic engagement, resilience-building dialogues, and advocacy for social justice to empower clients amidst societal turbulence.

This bonus chapter explores how mental health coaches adapt to emerging societal issues, leveraging evidence-based strategies and innovative approaches to promote resilience, well-being, and adaptive coping in clients facing contemporary mental health challenges. Coaches play a pivotal role in addressing these complexities, fostering personal growth, and empowering individuals to thrive amidst societal changes.

Bonus Chapter 8: Innovative Coaching Models

In response to evolving client needs and advancements in psychology and technology, new coaching models and approaches continue to emerge, offering innovative solutions to enhance mental well-being and personal development. This chapter explores several cutting-edge coaching models and their effectiveness in meeting diverse client needs.

Neuroscience-Informed Coaching: Integrating insights from neuroscience, this model emphasizes understanding brain mechanisms underlying behavior change and mental health. Coaches utilize neuroscientific principles to enhance coaching outcomes, optimize cognitive functioning, and facilitate sustainable behavior modification.

Positive Psychology Coaching: Grounded in positive psychology principles, this approach focuses on fostering strengths, resilience, and flourishing in clients. Coaches employ interventions such as gratitude exercises, strengths assessments, and goal-setting techniques to cultivate positive emotions and life satisfaction.

Narrative Coaching: Using storytelling techniques, narrative coaching helps clients reframe their personal narratives, identify core values, and align life choices with their authentic identities. Coaches facilitate reflective dialogue, narrative exploration, and meaning-making processes to empower clients in creating purposeful life narratives.

Solution-Focused Coaching: Centered on identifying and amplifying client strengths and resources, solution-focused coaching emphasizes practical solutions to achieve desired outcomes. Coaches employ goal-oriented conversations, scaling questions, and miracle question techniques to catalyze change and achieve sustainable results.

Behavioral Change Coaching: Drawing from behavioral science principles, this model targets habit formation, behavior modification, and goal attainment. Coaches apply behavioral change techniques such as reinforcement strategies, habit stacking, and environmental design to facilitate sustainable behavior change and promote long-term success.

Integrative Wellness Coaching: Holistically addressing physical, emotional, and spiritual dimensions of well-being, integrative wellness coaching integrates lifestyle medicine, holistic health practices, and mindfulness techniques. Coaches support clients in optimizing health behaviors, enhancing resilience, and fostering overall wellness through personalized coaching plans.

Mindfulness-Based Coaching: Rooted in mindfulness practices, this model cultivates present-moment awareness, self-compassion, and emotional regulation. Coaches guide clients in mindfulness meditation, mindful eating, and stress reduction techniques to enhance mental clarity, emotional well-being, and holistic self-care.

Virtual Reality (VR) Coaching: Leveraging immersive technology, VR coaching provides simulated environments for experiential learning, exposure therapy, and skill development. Coaches utilize VR platforms to enhance self-confidence, manage phobias, and practice social skills in safe, controlled settings.

Cultural Competence Coaching: Acknowledging cultural diversity and intersectional identities, cultural competence coaching tailors interventions to honor clients' cultural backgrounds, values, and lived experiences. Coaches promote inclusivity, cultural humility, and sensitivity in coaching interactions to foster trust and empower diverse client populations.

AI-Enhanced Coaching: Integrating artificial intelligence and machine learning algorithms, AI-enhanced coaching delivers personalized insights, behavior analytics, and adaptive coaching interventions. Coaches leverage AI-powered platforms for data-driven assessments, virtual coaching support, and real-time feedback to optimize client engagement and outcomes.

Each innovative coaching model offers distinct methodologies and evidence-based practices to address contemporary challenges and support holistic client growth. Coaches adapt these models to meet evolving client needs, promote positive change, and empower individuals in achieving their personal and professional aspirations.

Bonus Chapter 9: Long-term Impact and Sustainability:

What longitudinal studies or evidence exist regarding the long-term impact of coaching on mental health outcomes and sustainability?

Research on the long-term impact of coaching on mental health outcomes and sustainability is an evolving area, with several studies highlighting significant findings:

Sustained Behavioral Changes: Longitudinal studies indicate that coaching interventions can lead to sustained behavioral changes in areas such as stress management, goal attainment, and emotional regulation. Clients often report continued use of skills learned in coaching sessions, contributing to ongoing mental well-being.

Improved Psychological Resilience: Coaching has been linked to enhanced psychological resilience over time. Clients demonstrate improved coping mechanisms, reduced vulnerability to stressors, and increased adaptability in managing life challenges, fostering long-term mental health resilience.

Career and Personal Development: Evidence suggests that coaching supports sustained career advancement and personal growth. Clients maintain progress in achieving professional goals, navigating career transitions, and enhancing self-efficacy through ongoing coaching support.

Enhanced Quality of Life: Long-term coaching outcomes include improvements in overall quality of life indicators such as life satisfaction, interpersonal relationships, and subjective well-being. Clients report sustained benefits in self-awareness, fulfillment, and purposeful living.

Health Behavior Changes: Coaching interventions contribute to sustained improvements in health behaviors, including exercise adherence, dietary habits, and sleep patterns. Longitudinal studies highlight the role of coaching in promoting long-term lifestyle changes that support physical and mental health.

Cost-Effectiveness and Sustainability: Research underscores the cost-effectiveness and sustainability of coaching interventions in healthcare settings. Long-term studies demonstrate potential savings in healthcare utilization, reduced absenteeism, and improved workplace productivity associated with enhanced mental health outcomes.

Client Satisfaction and Engagement: High levels of client satisfaction and engagement contribute to the long-term effectiveness of coaching. Longitudinal research emphasizes the importance of the coaching relationship, personalized interventions, and client-centered approaches in achieving sustained outcomes.

Overall, longitudinal evidence supports the enduring impact of coaching on mental health outcomes, sustainability of behavior change, and holistic well-being across diverse client populations. Continued research advances our understanding of the long-term benefits of coaching and informs best practices for promoting enduring mental health resilience and personal growth.

Bonus Chapter 10: Professional Development and Education

As the field of coaching continues to evolve, future trends in coaching education and certification are shaping the preparation and professional development of aspiring coaches. This chapter explores emerging themes and strategies for navigating the landscape:

Specialized Certification Programs: Increasing demand for specialized coaching niches (e.g., executive coaching, health coaching) is driving the development of targeted certification programs. Aspiring coaches can benefit from accredited programs that offer comprehensive training, mentorship, and practical experience in their chosen specialty.

Integration of Technology: Educational programs are integrating technology-driven learning platforms, virtual classrooms, and AI-enhanced simulations to enhance coaching education. Aspiring coaches are encouraged to engage with digital tools, online resources, and virtual coaching environments to expand their skill set and adapt to technological advancements.

Evidence-Based Practices: Emphasis on evidence-based coaching methodologies and research-backed interventions is becoming integral to certification programs. Coaches are encouraged to stay abreast of current research, participate in continuing education, and apply empirical findings to enhance client outcomes and professional credibility.

Ethical Standards and Regulatory Compliance: Increasing regulatory scrutiny and ethical standards in coaching necessitate comprehensive education on ethical guidelines, client confidentiality, and professional conduct. Certification bodies and educational institutions are aligning curriculum with industry standards to ensure ethical practice and regulatory compliance.

Continuing Professional Development (CPD): Lifelong learning and CPD initiatives are essential for maintaining coaching credentials and staying competitive in the field. Aspiring coaches are advised to pursue ongoing education, attend workshops, and seek mentorship to deepen expertise, expand networks, and foster career longevity.

Globalization of Coaching: With coaching expanding globally, understanding cultural nuances, international coaching standards, and global best practices is crucial. Education programs are incorporating cross-cultural competencies, diversity training, and international perspectives to prepare coaches for diverse client demographics and global market demands.

Business Acumen and Entrepreneurship: Increasing emphasis on business acumen and entrepreneurship equips coaches with essential skills in marketing, client acquisition, and business management. Educational programs are integrating modules on practice building, client retention strategies, and financial planning to empower coaches as successful entrepreneurs.

By embracing these future-oriented trends and investing in robust education and certification pathways, aspiring coaches can cultivate a competitive edge, foster professional growth, and contribute to the advancement of the coaching profession globally.

Advanced Topics:

Trauma-Informed Coaching: Advanced techniques in trauma-informed coaching focus on creating a safe and supportive environment for clients who have experienced trauma. This approach emphasizes understanding the impact of trauma on the brain and behavior, fostering trust and empowerment, and integrating trauma-sensitive practices into coaching sessions.

Coaching for Chronic Illnesses: Techniques for coaching individuals with chronic illnesses involve understanding the unique challenges, emotional impacts, and lifestyle adjustments associated with long-term health conditions. Coaches may emphasize goal-setting tailored to health management, stress reduction strategies, resilience-building techniques, and collaboration with healthcare providers.

Mindfulness-Based Coaching: Advanced techniques in mindfulness-based coaching integrate mindfulness practices into coaching sessions to enhance self-awareness, emotional regulation, and stress management. Coaches may incorporate mindfulness exercises, meditation techniques, and cognitive restructuring to support clients in developing mindfulness skills for improved well-being.

Positive Psychology Interventions: Building on positive psychology principles, advanced coaching techniques focus on cultivating strengths, fostering optimism, and promoting resilience in clients. Coaches may use interventions such as gratitude practices, strengths assessments, and goal-oriented approaches to enhance positive emotions and psychological well-being.

Cognitive Behavioral Coaching (CBC): Advanced CBC techniques apply cognitive behavioral principles to help clients identify and modify negative thought patterns, behaviors, and emotional responses. Coaches may utilize cognitive restructuring, behavior activation, and problem-solving strategies to support clients in achieving behavioral change and improving mental health outcomes.

Existential Coaching: Techniques in existential coaching explore clients' search for meaning, purpose, and identity. Coaches may facilitate reflective dialogues, explore existential themes, and guide clients in making meaningful choices aligned with their values and life goals.

Group Coaching Dynamics: Advanced techniques in group coaching focus on facilitating group dynamics, promoting peer support, and fostering collaborative learning among participants. Coaches may use group exercises, role-playing, and feedback sessions to enhance interpersonal skills, collective problem-solving, and mutual accountability within the group setting.

These advanced techniques are tailored to address specific mental health challenges and client populations, offering coaches a diversified toolkit to support individuals in achieving their personal and therapeutic goals effectively.

Neuroscience and Behavior Change: Insights from neuroscience continue to evolve understanding of how brain functions influence behavior change and mental health outcomes. Readers would benefit from updates on neuroscientific research related to coaching interventions.

Psychological Interventions: Advances in psychology provide new techniques and approaches for coaching, such as cognitive-behavioral, positive psychology, and mindfulness-based interventions. Readers may seek updates on the efficacy and application of these interventions in coaching practice.

Health and Well-being: Research on lifestyle factors, health behaviors, and their impact on mental health is of interest to coaches supporting clients in achieving holistic well-being. Updates on integrative approaches combining physical health and mental health coaching would be valuable.

Technology and Digital Platforms: Innovations in technology, including AI, virtual reality, and telehealth platforms, are shaping coaching practices. Readers may want to explore research on how these technologies enhance coaching effectiveness, client engagement, and accessibility.

Cultural Competence and Diversity: Research on cultural influences, diversity considerations, and culturally competent coaching practices is essential for coaches working with diverse client populations. Updates on effective strategies and best practices in cultural competence would be beneficial.

Longitudinal Studies and Outcomes: Long-term studies examining the sustained impact of coaching interventions on client outcomes provide valuable insights into the effectiveness and durability of coaching approaches. Readers may seek updates on longitudinal research findings in mental health coaching.

Professional Ethics and Standards: Evolving ethical standards and best practices in coaching require continual updates based on research and industry developments. Readers would benefit from updates on ethical considerations, boundaries, and professional standards in coaching practice.

Client-Centered Outcomes: Research focusing on client perspectives, satisfaction, and outcomes in coaching interventions helps validate coaching effectiveness and guides evidence-based practice. Readers may be interested in studies exploring client-reported outcomes and experiences.

By staying informed about the latest research findings and evidence-based practices, mental health coaches can enhance their knowledge, skills, and effectiveness in supporting clients' mental and emotional well-being.

Case Studies in Specific Mental Health Challenges: Detailed case studies focusing on anxiety disorders, depression, substance abuse, trauma recovery, and other mental health issues can provide coaches with insights into effective coaching strategies, client progress over time, and outcomes achieved.

Client-Centered Approaches: Case studies illustrating client-centered coaching approaches, where the coach tailors their methods to meet the unique needs and goals of individual clients, can demonstrate the versatility and efficacy of coaching in various contexts.

Cultural and Diversity Considerations: Case studies highlighting coaching sessions with diverse populations, including different cultural backgrounds, LGBTQ+ individuals, and varying socioeconomic statuses, can illustrate the importance of cultural competence and sensitivity in coaching practices.

Integration of Different Coaching Models: Case studies showcasing the integration of different coaching models, such as cognitive-behavioral coaching, positive psychology interventions, mindfulness-based approaches, and existential coaching, can demonstrate the flexibility and effectiveness of these methodologies.

Longitudinal Case Studies: Long-term case studies tracking client progress and outcomes over extended periods can provide insights into the sustainability of coaching interventions and the long-term impact on clients' lives.

Success Stories and Testimonials: Real-life success stories and testimonials from clients who have benefited from coaching can inspire readers and provide concrete examples of coaching effectiveness in achieving personal growth, resilience, and improved mental health.

Challenges and Solutions: Case studies that address challenges encountered during coaching sessions, such as resistance to change, setbacks in progress, or ethical dilemmas, can offer valuable lessons and strategies for overcoming obstacles in coaching practice.

By incorporating practical examples and case studies into their learning, mental health coaches can gain a deeper understanding of how theoretical concepts translate into real-world coaching scenarios. This enables them to develop their skills, enhance client outcomes, and contribute effectively to the field of mental health coaching.

Professional Development and Continuing Education
1. Introduction to Professional Development
Importance of Lifelong Learning: Emphasizing the role of continuous education in maintaining competence and adapting to evolving client needs.
Benefits of Professional Development: Discussing how ongoing learning enhances coaching effectiveness and client outcomes.
2. Continuing Education Opportunities
Formal Education Programs: Overview of accredited coaching programs, certifications, and degrees relevant to mental health coaching.
Continuing Education Units (CEUs): Exploring options for obtaining CEUs through workshops, seminars, and online courses.
Specialized Training: Resources for gaining expertise in specific areas such as trauma-informed coaching, addiction recovery, or coaching for chronic illnesses.
3. Career Advancement Strategies
Career Pathways in Coaching: Discussing potential roles and career trajectories within the coaching profession.
Building a Coaching Practice: Guidance on starting a private practice, marketing strategies, and client acquisition.
Advanced Coaching Roles: Exploring opportunities in organizational coaching, executive coaching, or consulting roles.
4. Professional Development Resources
Industry Associations and Networks: Listing professional organizations and networks for mental health coaches.
Mentorship and Supervision: Importance of mentorship and supervision in professional growth and skill development.
Peer Support Groups: Benefits of joining peer support groups or mastermind circles for ongoing learning and collaboration.
5. Ethical Considerations in Professional Development
Maintaining Ethical Standards: Integrating ethical guidelines into professional development activities.

Confidentiality and Boundaries: Ensuring ethical practice in educational and career advancement contexts.
Legal Implications: Understanding legal responsibilities related to coaching practice and professional development activities.
6. Personal Growth and Well-being
Self-Care Practices: Importance of self-care for sustaining long-term success in coaching.
Managing Burnout: Strategies for preventing and managing burnout in a demanding profession.
Balancing Professional and Personal Life: Tips for maintaining work-life balance while pursuing professional development.
7. Future Trends and Innovations
Emerging Trends: Exploration of new methodologies, technologies, and research shaping the future of mental health coaching.
Innovative Approaches: Examples of innovative coaching techniques or modalities gaining traction in the field.
Adapting to Change: Strategies for staying ahead of industry trends and adapting to changing client needs.

1. Introduction to Cultural Competence in Coaching
Understanding Cultural Diversity
Cultural competence begins with an awareness and understanding of the diversity of cultural backgrounds that clients may come from. This includes recognizing differences in beliefs, values, traditions, communication styles, and worldviews. Coaches must appreciate that these cultural factors significantly influence how individuals perceive and address mental health challenges.

Benefits of Cultural Awareness
Embracing cultural sensitivity enhances the therapeutic alliance between coach and client. By respecting and understanding cultural differences, coaches can establish trust more easily, communicate effectively, and tailor interventions to meet the specific needs of clients. This approach not only improves client satisfaction but also increases the likelihood of positive outcomes in coaching sessions.

2. Cultural Influences on Mental Health
Cultural Factors in Mental Health
Culture profoundly shapes attitudes towards mental health, help-seeking behaviors, and the stigma associated with mental disorders. For instance, certain cultures may prioritize family support over individual therapy, or have distinct beliefs about the causes of mental illness (e.g., spiritual, supernatural). Coaches need to be sensitive to these cultural nuances to provide effective support.

Impact of Intersectionality

Intersectionality acknowledges that individuals hold multiple social identities (e.g., race, gender, sexual orientation, socioeconomic status) that intersect and influence their experiences. Coaches must consider how these intersecting identities impact mental health needs and preferences for coaching approaches. This awareness helps coaches tailor their interventions more effectively to address diverse client needs.

3. Coaching Practices in Different Cultural Contexts
Case Studies
Examining case studies where cultural competence was successfully integrated into coaching can provide valuable insights. These examples illustrate how coaches adapted their techniques to align with cultural norms, values, and communication styles, ultimately leading to improved client engagement and outcomes.

Cultural Competence in Action
Practical strategies for coaches include using culturally appropriate language, respecting rituals or customs important to clients, and being open to learning about different cultural perspectives. Coaches should approach each client as an individual within their cultural context, fostering a collaborative and respectful coaching relationship.

4. Enhancing Cultural Competence
Training and Education
Ongoing professional development is essential for coaches to enhance their cultural competence. Training programs, workshops, and certifications focused on cultural awareness and sensitivity can provide coaches with the knowledge and skills needed to effectively navigate diverse cultural contexts.

Self-Reflection and Awareness

Coaches should engage in self-assessment to identify personal biases, assumptions, and stereotypes that may affect their coaching practice. This introspective process helps coaches develop a deeper understanding of their own cultural identity and biases, enabling them to better support clients from diverse backgrounds.

5. Addressing Challenges in Cross-Cultural Coaching
Communication Barriers
Language differences can pose significant challenges in coaching sessions. Coaches may need to use interpreters or translators proficient in both languages to ensure clear and accurate communication. Additionally, coaches should adapt their communication style to accommodate varying levels of language proficiency among clients.

Navigating Cultural Differences
Coaches must navigate differences in values, beliefs, and expectations regarding mental health and coaching. This includes addressing potential conflicts that may arise due to cultural disparities and finding respectful ways to resolve them while upholding ethical standards and maintaining client trust.

6. Ethics and Cultural Sensitivity
Ethical Considerations
Ethical guidelines for coaching emphasize the importance of cultural competence in providing ethical and effective services. Coaches must uphold principles of respect, confidentiality, and non-discrimination in all interactions with clients from diverse cultural backgrounds.

Respecting Diversity

Coaches should prioritize inclusivity and respect for diversity in their coaching practice. This involves valuing and incorporating clients' cultural perspectives and preferences into coaching interventions, ensuring that coaching strategies align with clients' cultural identities and values.

7. Global Best Practices in Mental Health Coaching

International Perspectives

Learning from global leaders in mental health coaching provides insights into effective strategies and best practices across different cultural settings. Coaches can adapt successful coaching models from diverse global contexts to meet the unique needs of clients in their own cultural environments.

Adapting to Local Contexts

Effective coaching requires an understanding of local cultural, social, and economic factors that influence mental health and help-seeking behaviors. Coaches should be flexible in their approach, adapting evidence-based practices to align with the specific cultural context of their clients.

8. Conclusion and Call to Action

Importance of Cultural Competence

Cultural competence is essential for enhancing client engagement, improving coaching outcomes, and promoting mental well-being across diverse populations. Coaches play a pivotal role in fostering cultural sensitivity and advocating for inclusive practices in mental health coaching.

Continued Learning

Coaches are encouraged to pursue ongoing education and professional development in cultural competence. This includes attending workshops, engaging in cultural humility training, and seeking mentorship opportunities to further enhance their skills and knowledge.

Case Study 1: Addressing Cultural Stigma
Client Background: Maria, a Latina immigrant, seeks coaching to manage stress and improve work-life balance. She values family support but feels conflicted about seeking help due to cultural stigma surrounding mental health issues in her community.

Coaching Approach: The coach acknowledges Maria's cultural values and emphasizes the importance of self-care within a family context. They explore stress management techniques that align with Maria's cultural beliefs, such as incorporating family activities into relaxation routines. The coach also addresses stigma by normalizing discussions about mental health within Maria's cultural framework, emphasizing strength and resilience in seeking support.

Outcome: Maria feels empowered to prioritize her well-being while honoring her cultural values. She becomes more open to discussing mental health with her family and seeks ongoing coaching to navigate challenges while maintaining cultural authenticity.

Case Study 2: Cross-Cultural Communication
Client Background: Ahmad, a Middle Eastern student studying abroad, experiences anxiety and difficulty adjusting to a new cultural environment. He seeks coaching to build confidence and develop strategies for academic success.

Coaching Approach: The coach recognizes Ahmad's cultural background and language barriers as potential communication challenges. They use culturally sensitive language and visual aids to facilitate understanding. The coach incorporates Ahmad's cultural values of respect for authority and community support into goal-setting exercises, encouraging him to leverage his cultural strengths in academic settings.

Outcome: Ahmad gains confidence and develops effective study habits tailored to his cultural preferences. He feels more integrated into his academic environment and continues coaching to further enhance his personal and academic growth.

Case Study 3: LGBTQ+ Cultural Competence
Client Background: Jamie, a non-binary individual, seeks coaching to navigate workplace challenges related to identity acceptance and career advancement. They express concerns about workplace inclusivity and fear of discrimination.

Coaching Approach: The coach demonstrates cultural competence by respecting Jamie's gender identity and using inclusive language throughout coaching sessions. They explore strategies for navigating workplace dynamics while affirming Jamie's identity and promoting self-advocacy. The coach collaborates with Jamie to identify supportive resources and networks within the LGBTQ+ community that align with their career goals.

Outcome: Jamie feels empowered to advocate for themselves in the workplace and develops a clearer career path that integrates their identity and professional aspirations. They experience increased job satisfaction and continue coaching to address new challenges and opportunities.

These case studies illustrate how cultural competence in coaching involves understanding and respecting clients' cultural backgrounds, adapting coaching approaches accordingly, and fostering a supportive environment that honors diversity and promotes positive client outcomes.

Coaching Children and Adolescents
Approach:

Client Background: Emma, a 13-year-old student, struggles with academic pressure and social anxiety. Her parents seek coaching to help her build confidence and manage stress effectively.

Coaching Approach: The coach uses age-appropriate techniques such as storytelling, art therapy, and play-based activities to engage Emma. They focus on building resilience, emotional regulation skills, and effective communication strategies. The coach collaborates closely with Emma's parents and teachers to create a supportive environment that reinforces coaching goals.

Outcome: Emma develops stronger coping mechanisms, improves academic performance, and feels more confident in social situations. Her parents notice positive changes in her behavior and continue coaching to support Emma's ongoing growth and development.

Coaching Older Adults
Approach:

Client Background: John, a retired professional in his 70s, experiences feelings of loneliness and loss of purpose after retiring. He seeks coaching to explore new interests and maintain a fulfilling lifestyle.

Coaching Approach: The coach acknowledges John's life experience and focuses on identifying meaningful activities and goals aligned with his values and interests. They incorporate reminiscence therapy to reflect on past achievements and strengths. The coach supports John in exploring volunteer opportunities, social groups, and lifelong learning programs tailored to older adults.

Outcome: John renews his sense of purpose, finds fulfillment in new hobbies and social connections, and maintains mental and emotional well-being in retirement. He continues coaching to navigate life transitions and embrace opportunities for personal growth.

Coaching LGBTQ+ Individuals
Approach:

Client Background: Alex, a transgender individual, seeks coaching to navigate workplace challenges and explore career advancement opportunities while affirming their identity.

Coaching Approach: The coach demonstrates cultural competence by using inclusive language and understanding the unique challenges faced by LGBTQ+ individuals in professional settings. They collaborate with Alex to develop strategies for workplace advocacy, networking within LGBTQ+ communities, and overcoming bias and discrimination. The coach integrates personal identity affirmation and career development goals into coaching sessions.

Outcome: Alex gains confidence in advocating for their rights and career aspirations, achieves professional milestones aligned with their values, and fosters a supportive workplace environment. They continue coaching to navigate career transitions and maintain career satisfaction.

Coaching for Other Specific Demographics
Approach:

Client Background: Sarah, a single parent juggling multiple responsibilities, seeks coaching to achieve work-life balance and manage stress effectively.

Coaching Approach: The coach acknowledges Sarah's unique challenges as a single parent and collaborates with her to prioritize self-care, time management strategies, and goal-setting techniques. They explore resources and support networks for single parents, emphasizing resilience-building and emotional well-being.

Outcome: Sarah improves time management skills, reduces stress levels, and experiences greater satisfaction in balancing her personal and professional responsibilities. She continues coaching to sustain positive changes and navigate new challenges.

These tailored coaching approaches illustrate how understanding demographic-specific needs and using appropriate coaching techniques can support clients in achieving their goals, fostering resilience, and enhancing overall well-being.